DATE DUE

Approaches and methods
in language teaching

CAMBRIDGE LANGUAGE TEACHING LIBRARY
A series of authoritative books on subjects of central importance for all
language teachers.

In this series:

Teaching and Learning Languages *by Earl W. Stevick*

Communicating Naturally in a Second Language – Theory and practice in
language teaching *by Wilga M. Rivers*

Speaking in Many Tongues – Essays in foreign language teaching
by Wilga M. Rivers

Teaching the Spoken Language – An approach based on the analysis of
conversational English *by Gillian Brown and George Yule*

A Foundation Course for Language Teachers *by Tom McArthur*

Foreign and Second Language Learning – Language acquisition research
and its implications for the classroom *by William Littlewood*

Communicative Methodology in Language Teaching – The roles of fluency
and accuracy *by Christopher Brumfit*

The Context of Language Teaching *by Jack C. Richards*

English for Science and Technology – A discourse approach
by Louis Trimble

Approaches and Methods in Language Teaching – A description and
analysis *by Jack C. Richards and Theodore S. Rodgers*

Images and Options in the Language Classroom *by Earl W. Stevick*

Culture Bound – Bridging the cultural gap in language teaching
edited by Joyce Merrill Valdes

Interactive Language Teaching *edited by Wilga M. Rivers*

Approaches and Methods in Language Teaching

A description and analysis

Jack C. Richards and Theodore S. Rodgers

University of Hawaii

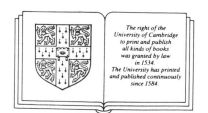

The right of the
University of Cambridge
to print and publish
all kinds of books
was granted by law
in 1534.
The University has printed
and published continuously
since 1584.

Cambridge University Press
Cambridge
New York   New Rochelle
Melbourne   Sydney

Published by the Press Syndicate of the University of Cambridge
The Pitt Building, Trumpington Street, Cambridge CB2 1RP
32 East 57th Street, New York, NY 10022, USA
10 Stamford Road, Oakleigh, Melbourne 3166, Australia

First published 1986
Fourth printing 1988

Printed in the United States of America

Library of Congress Cataloging in Publication Data
Richards, Jack C.
Approaches and methods in language teaching.
(Cambridge language teaching library)
Includes bibliographies and index.
1. Language and languages – Study and teaching.
I. Rodgers, Theodore S. (Theodore Stephen),
1934–. II. Title. III. Series.
P51.R467   1986   418′.007   85–11698

British Library Cataloging in Publication Data
Richards, J.C. (Jack C.)
Approaches and methods in language teaching. –
(Cambridge language teaching library).
1. Language and languages – study and teaching
I. Title   II. Rodgers, Theodore S.
418′.007   P51

ISBN 0 521 32093 3 hardcover
ISBN 0 521 31255 8 paperback

Contents

Preface

The proliferation of approaches and methods is a prominent characteristic of contemporary second and foreign language teaching. To some,
this reflects the strength of our profession. Invention of new classroom
practices and approaches to designing language programs and materials
reflects a commitment to finding more efficient and more effective ways
of teaching languages. The classroom teacher and the program coor-
dinator have a wider variety of methodological options to choose from
than ever before. They can choose methods and materials according to
the needs of learners, the preferences of teachers, and the constraints of
the school or educational setting.

To others, however, the wide variety of method options currently
available confuses rather than comforts. Methods appear to be based
on very different views of what language is and how a language is
learned. Some methods recommend apparently strange and unfamiliar
classroom techniques and practices; others are described in books that
are hard to locate, obscurely written, and difficult to understand. Above
all, the practitioner is often bewildered by the lack of any comprehensive
theory of what an approach and method are. This book was written in
response to this situation. It is an attempt to depict, organize, and analyze
major and minor approaches and methods in language teaching, and to
describe their underlying nature.

Approaches and Methods in Language Teaching is designed to provide
a detailed account of major twentieth-century trends in language teaching. To highlight the similarities and differences between approaches
and methods, the same descriptive framework is used throughout. This
model is presented in Chapter 2 and is used in subsequent chapters. It
describes approaches and methods according to their underlying theories
of language and language learning; the learning objectives; the syllabus
model used; the roles of teachers, learners, and materials within the
method or approach; and the classroom procedures and techniques that
the method uses. Where a method or approach has extensive and acknowledged links to a particular tradition in second or foreign language
teaching, this historical background is treated in the first section of the
chapter. Where an approach or method has no acknowledged ties to
established second or foreign language teaching practice, historical perspective is not relevant. In these cases the method is considered in terms

of its links to more general linguistic, psychological, or educational traditions.

Within each chapter, our aim has been to present an objective and comprehensive picture of a particular approach or method. We have avoided personal evaluation, preferring to let the method speak for itself and allow readers to make their own appraisals. The book is not intended to popularize or promote particular approaches or methods, nor is it an attempt to train teachers in the use of the different methods described. Rather it is designed to give the teacher or teacher trainee a straightforward introduction to commonly used and less commonly used methods, and a set of criteria by which to critically read, question, and observe methods. In the final chapter we examine methods from a broader framework and present a curriculum-development perspective on methodology. Limitations of method claims are discussed, and the need for evaluation and research is emphasized. We hope that the analysis of approaches and methods presented here will elevate the level of discussion found in the methods literature, which sometimes has a polemical and promotional quality. Our goal is to enable teachers to become better informed about the nature, strengths, and weaknesses of methods and approaches so they can better arrive at their own judgments and decisions.

Portions of Chapter 2 are based on Jack C. Richards and Theodore Rodgers, "Method: approach, design, procedure," *TESOL Quarterly* 16(2): 153–68. We would like to thank the following people for their assistance in the preparation of this manuscript: Eileen Cain for Chapter 6; Jonathan Hull, Deborah Gordon, and Joel Wiskin for Chapter 7; Graham Crookes and Phillip Hull for Chapter 8; and Peter Halpern and Unise Lange for Chapter 9. We would like to acknowledge especially the editorial skills of our editor, Sandra Graham of Cambridge University Press.

1   A brief history of language teaching

This chapter, in briefly reviewing the history of language teaching methods, provides a background for discussion of contemporary methods and suggests the issues we will refer to in analyzing these methods. From this historical perspective we are also able to see that the concerns that have prompted modern method innovations were similar to those that have always been at the center of discussions on how to teach foreign languages. Changes in language teaching methods throughout history have reflected recognition of changes in the kind of proficiency learners need, such as a move toward oral proficiency rather than reading comprehension as the goal of language study; they have also reflected changes in theories of the nature of language and of language learning. Kelly (1969) and Howatt (1984) have demonstrated that many current issues in language teaching are not particularly new. Today's controversies reflect contemporary responses to questions that have been asked often throughout the history of language teaching.

It has been estimated that some sixty percent of today's world population is multilingual. Both from a contemporary and a historical perspective, bilingualism or multilingualism is the norm rather than the exception. It is fair, then, to say that throughout history foreign language learning has always been an important practical concern. Whereas today English is the world's most widely studied foreign language, five hundred years ago it was Latin, for it was the dominant language of education, commerce, religion, and government in the Western world. In the sixteenth century, however, French, Italian, and English gained in importance as a result of political changes in Europe, and Latin gradually became displaced as a language of spoken and written communication.

As the status of Latin diminished from that of a living language to that of an "occasional" subject in the school curriculum, the study of Latin took on a different function. The study of classical Latin (the Latin in which the classical works of Virgil, Ovid, and Cicero were written) and an analysis of its grammar and rhetoric became the model for foreign language study from the seventeenth to the nineteenth centuries. Children entering "grammar school" in the sixteenth, seventeenth, and eighteenth centuries in England were initially given a rigorous introduction to Latin grammar, which was taught through rote learning of grammar rules, study of declensions and conjugations, translation, and practice in writing sample sentences, sometimes with the use of parallel bilingual texts and dialogue (Kelly 1969; Howatt 1983). Once basic proficiency was established, students were introduced to the advanced study of grammar and rhetoric. School learning must have been a deadening experience for children, for lapses in knowledge were often met with brutal punishment. There were occasional attempts to promote alternative approaches to education; Roger Ascham and Montaigne in the sixteenth century and Comenius and John Locke in the seventeenth century, for example, had made specific proposals for curriculum reform and for changes in the way Latin was taught (Kelly 1969; Howatt 1984), but since Latin (and, to a lesser extent, Greek) had for so long been regarded as the classical and therefore most ideal form of language, it was not surprising that ideas about the role of language study in the curriculum reflected the long-established status of Latin.

The decline of Latin also brought with it a new justification for teaching Latin. Latin was said to develop intellectual abilities, and the study of Latin grammar became an end in itself.

When once the Latin tongue had ceased to be a normal vehicle for communication, and was replaced as such by the vernacular languages, then it most speedily became a 'mental gymnastic', the supremely 'dead' language, a disciplined and systematic study of which was held to be indispensable as a basis for all forms of higher education. (V. Mallison, cited in Titone 1968: 26)

As "modern" languages began to enter the curriculum of European schools in the eighteenth century, they were taught using the same basic procedures that were used for teaching Latin. Textbooks consisted of statements of abstract grammar rules, lists of vocabulary, and sentences for translation. Speaking the foreign language was not the goal, and oral practice was limited to students reading aloud the sentences they had translated. These sentences were constructed to illustrate the grammatical system of the language and consequently bore no relation to the language of real communication. Students labored over translating sentences like the following:

The philosopher pulled the lower jaw of the hen.
My sons have bought the mirrors of the Duke.
The cat of my aunt is more treacherous than the dog of your uncle.
(Titone 1968: 28)

By the nineteenth century, this approach based on the study of Latin had become the standard way of studying foreign languages in schools. A typical textbook in the mid-nineteenth century thus consisted of chapters or lessons organized around grammar points. Each grammar point was listed, rules on its use were explained, and it was illustrated by sample sentences.

2

Nineteenth-century textbook compilers were mainly determined to codify the foreign language into frozen rules of morphology and syntax to be explained and eventually memorized. Oral work was reduced to an absolute minimum, while a handful of written exercises, constructed at random, came as a sort of appendix to the rules. Of the many books published during this period, those by Seidenstücker and Plötz were perhaps the most typical... [Seidenstücker] reduced the material to disconnected sentences to illustrate specific rules. He divided his text carefully into two parts, one giving the rules and necessary paradigms, the other giving French sentences for translation into German and German sentences for translation into French. The immediate aim was for the student to apply the given rules by means of appropriate exercises... In [Plötz's] textbooks, divided into the two parts described above, the sole form of instruction was mechanical translation. Typical sentences were: 'Thou hast a book. The house is beautiful. He has a kind dog. We have a bread [sic]. The door is black. He has a book and a dog. The horse of the father was kind.' (Titone 1968: 27)

This approach to foreign language teaching became known as the Grammar-Translation Method.

The Grammar-Translation Method

As the names of some of its leading exponents suggest (Johann Seidenstücker, Karl Plötz, H. S. Ollendorf, and Johann Meidinger), Grammar Translation was the offspring of German scholarship, the object of which, according to one of its less charitable critics, was "to know everything about something rather than the thing itself" (W. H. D. Rouse, quoted in Kelly 1969: 53). Grammar Translation was in fact first known in the United States as the Prussian Method. (A book by B. Sears, an American classics teacher, published in 1845 was entitled *The Ciceronian or the Prussian Method of Teaching the Elements of the Latin Language* [Kelly 1969].) The principal characteristics of the Grammar-Translation Method were these:

1. The goal of foreign language study is to learn a language in order to read its literature or in order to benefit from the mental discipline and intellectual development that result from foreign-language study. Grammar Translation is a way of studying a language that approaches the language first through detailed analysis of its grammar rules, followed by application of this knowledge to the task of translating sentences and texts into and out of the target language. It hence views language learning as consisting of little more than memorizing rules and facts in order to understand and manipulate the morphology and syntax of the foreign language. "The first language is maintained as the reference system in the acquisition of the second language" (Stern 1983: 455).

2. Reading and writing are the major focus; little or no systematic attention is paid to speaking or listening.

3

3. Vocabulary selection is based solely on the reading texts used, and words are taught through bilingual word lists, dictionary study, and memorization. In a typical Grammar-Translation text, the grammar rules are presented and illustrated, a list of vocabulary items are presented with their translation equivalents, and translation exercises are prescribed.
4. The sentence is the basic unit of teaching and language practice. Much of the lesson is devoted to translating sentences into and out of the target language, and it is this focus on the sentence that is a distinctive feature of the method. Earlier approaches to foreign language study used grammar as an aid to the study of texts in a foreign language. But this was thought to be too difficult for students in secondary schools, and the focus on the sentence was an attempt to make language learning easier (see Howatt 1984: 131).
5. Accuracy is emphasized. Students are expected to attain high standards in translation, because of "the high priority attached to meticulous standards of accuracy which, as well as having an intrinsic moral value, was a prerequisite for passing the increasing number of formal written examinations that grew up during the century" (Howatt 1984: 132).
6. Grammar is taught deductively – that is, by presentation and study of grammar rules, which are then practiced through translation exercises. In most Grammar-Translation texts, a syllabus was followed for the sequencing of grammar points throughout a text, and there was an attempt to teach grammar in an organized and systematic way.
7. The student's native language is the medium of instruction. It is used to explain new items and to enable comparisons to be made between the foreign language and the student's native language.

Grammar Translation dominated European and foreign language teaching from the 1840s to the 1940s, and in modified form it continues to be widely used in some parts of the world today. At its best, as Howatt (1984) points out, it was not necessarily the horror that its critics depicted it as. Its worst excesses were introduced by those who wanted to demonstrate that the study of French or German was no less rigorous than the study of classical languages. This resulted in the type of Grammar-Translation courses remembered with distaste by thousands of school learners, for whom foreign language learning meant a tedious experience of memorizing endless lists of unusable grammar rules and vocabulary and attempting to produce perfect translations of stilted or literary prose. Although the Grammar-Translation Method often creates frustration for students, it makes few demands on teachers. It is still used in situations where understanding literary texts is the primary focus of foreign language study and there is little need for a speaking knowledge of the language. Contemporary texts for the teaching of foreign languages at college level often reflect Grammar-Translation principles. These texts are frequently the products of people trained in literature rather than in language teaching or applied linguistics. Consequently, though it may be true to say that the Grammar-Translation Method is still widely practiced, it has no advocates. It is a method for which there is no theory. There is no literature that offers a rationale or justification for it or that attempts to relate it to issues in linguistics, psychology, or educational theory.

In the mid- and late nineteenth century opposition to the Grammar-Translation Method gradually developed in several European countries. This Reform Movement, as it was referred to, laid the foundations for the development of new ways of teaching languages and raised controversies that have continued to the present day.

Language teaching innovations in the nineteenth century

Toward the mid-nineteenth century several factors contributed to a questioning and rejection of the Grammar-Translation Method. Increased opportunities for communication among Europeans created a demand for oral proficiency in foreign languages. Initially this created a market for conversation books and phrase books intended for private study, but language teaching specialists also turned their attention to the way modern languages were being taught in secondary schools. Increasingly the public education system was seen to be failing in its responsibilities. In Germany, England, France, and other parts of Europe, new approaches to language teaching were developed by individual language teaching specialists, each with a specific method for reforming the teaching of modern languages. Some of these specialists, like C. Marcel, T. Prendergast, and F. Gouin, did not manage to achieve any lasting impact, though their ideas are of historical interest.

The Frenchman C. Marcel (1793–1896) referred to child language learning as a model for language teaching, emphasized the importance of meaning in learning, proposed that reading be taught before other skills, and tried to locate language teaching within a broader educational framework. The Englishman T. Prendergast (1806–1886) was one of the first to record the observation that children use contextual and situational cues to interpret utterances and that they use memorized phrases and "routines" in speaking. He proposed the first "structural syllabus," advocating that learners be taught the most basic structural patterns occurring in the language. In this way he was anticipating an issue that was to be taken up in the 1920s and 1930s, as we shall see in Chapter 3. The Frenchman F. Gouin (1831–1896) is perhaps the best known of these mid-nineteenth century reformers. Gouin developed an approach to teaching a foreign language based on his observations of children's use of language. He believed that language learning was facilitated through using language to accomplish events consisting of a sequence of related actions. His method used situations and themes as ways of organizing and presenting oral language – the famous Gouin "series," which includes sequences of sentences related to such activities as chopping wood and opening the door. Gouin established schools to teach according to his method, and it was quite popular for a time. In the first lesson of a foreign language the following series would be learned:

I walk toward the door.	I walk.
I draw near to the door.	I draw near.
I draw nearer to the door.	I draw nearer.
I get to the door.	I get to.
I stop at the door.	I stop.
I stretch out my arm.	I stretch out.
I take hold of the handle.	I take hold.
I turn the handle.	I turn.
I open the door.	I open.
I pull the door.	I pull.
The door moves.	moves
The door turns on its hinges.	turns
The door turns and turns.	turns
I open the door wide.	I open.
I let go of the handle.	let go.

(Titone 1968: 35)

Gouin's emphasis on the need to present new teaching items in a context that makes their meaning clear, and the use of gestures and actions to convey the meanings of utterances, are practices that later became part of such approaches and methods as Situational Language Teaching (Chapter 3) and Total Physical Response (Chapter 6).

The work of individual language specialists like these reflects the changing climate of the times in which they worked. Educators recognized the need for speaking proficiency rather than reading comprehension, grammar, or literary appreciation as the goal for foreign language programs; there was an interest in how children learn languages, which prompted attempts to develop teaching principles from observation of (or more typically, reflections about) child language learning. But the ideas and methods of Marcel, Prendergast, Gouin, and other innovators were developed outside the context of established circles of education and hence lacked the means for wider dissemination, acceptance, and implementation. They were writing at a time when there was not sufficient organizational structure in the language teaching profession (i.e., in the form of professional associations, journals, and conferences) to enable new ideas to develop into an educational movement. This began to change toward the end of the nineteenth century, however, when a more concerted effort arose in which the interests of reform-minded language teachers, and linguists, coincided. Teachers and linguists began to write about the need for new approaches to language teaching, and through their pamphlets, books, speeches, and articles, the foundation for more widespread pedagogical reforms was laid. This effort became known as the Reform Movement in language teaching.

The Reform Movement

Language teaching specialists like Marcel, Prendergast, and Gouin had done much to promote alternative approaches to language teaching, but their ideas failed to receive widespread support or attention. From the 1880s, however, practically minded linguists like Henry Sweet in England, Wilhelm Viëtor in Germany, and Paul Passy in France began to provide the intellectual leadership needed to give reformist ideas greater credibility and acceptance. The discipline of linguistics was revitalized. Phonetics – the scientific analysis and description of the sound systems of languages – was established, giving new insights into speech processes. Linguists emphasized that speech, rather than the written word, was the primary form of language. The International Phonetic Association was founded in 1886, and its International Phonetic Alphabet (IPA) was designed to enable the sounds of any language to be accurately transcribed. One of the earliest goals of the association was to improve the teaching of modern languages. It advocated

1. the study of the spoken language;
2. phonetic training in order to establish good pronunciation habits;
3. the use of conversation texts and dialogues to introduce conversational phrases and idioms;
4. an inductive approach to the teaching of grammar;
5. teaching new meanings through establishing associations within the target language rather than by establishing associations with the mother tongue.

Linguists too became interested in the controversies that emerged about the best way to teach foreign languages, and ideas were fiercely discussed and defended in books, articles, and pamphlets. Henry Sweet (1845–1912) argued that sound methodological principles should be based on a scientific analysis of language and a study of psychology. In his book *The Practical Study of Languages* (1899) he set forth principles for the development of teaching method. These included

1. careful selection of what is to be taught;
2. imposing limits on what is to be taught;
3. arranging what is to be taught in terms of the four skills of listening, speaking, reading, and writing;
4. grading materials from simple to complex.

In Germany the prominent scholar Wilhelm Viëtor (1850–1918) used linguistic theory to justify his views on language teaching. He argued that training in phonetics would enable teachers to pronounce the language accurately. Speech patterns, rather than grammar, were the fundamental elements of language. In 1882 he published his views in an influential pamphlet, *Language Teaching Must Start Afresh*, in which he strongly criticized the inadequacies of Grammar Translation and stressed the value of training teachers in the new science of phonetics.

Viëtor, Sweet, and other reformers in the late nineteenth century shared many beliefs about the principles on which a new approach to teaching foreign languages should be based, although they often differed considerably in the specific procedures they advocated for teaching a language. In general the reformers believed that

1. the spoken language is primary and that this should be reflected in an oral-based methodology;
2. the findings of phonetics should be applied to teaching and to teacher training;
3. learners should hear the language first, before seeing it in written form;
4. words should be presented in sentences, and sentences should be practiced in meaningful contexts and not be taught as isolated, disconnected elements;
5. the rules of grammar should be taught only after the students have practiced the grammar points in context – that is, grammar should be taught inductively;
6. translation should be avoided, although the mother tongue could be used in order to explain new words or to check comprehension.

These principles provided the theoretical foundations for a principled approach to language teaching, one based on a scientific approach to the study of language and of language learning. They reflect the beginnings of the discipline of applied linguistics – that branch of language study concerned with the scientific study of second and foreign language teaching and learning. The writings of such scholars as Sweet, Viëtor, and Passy provided suggestions on how these applied linguistic principles could best be put into practice. None of these proposals assumed the status of a method, however, in the sense of a widely recognized and uniformly implemented design for teaching a language. But parallel to the ideas put forward by members of the Reform Movement was an interest in developing principles for language teaching out of naturalistic principles of language learning, such as are seen in first language acquisition. This led to what have been termed *natural methods* and ultimately led to the development of what came to be known as the Direct Method.

The Direct Method

Gouin had been one of the first of the nineteenth-century reformers to attempt to build a methodology around observation of child language learning. Other reformers toward the end of the century likewise turned their attention to naturalistic principles of language learning, and for this reason they are sometimes referred to as advocates of a "natural" method. In fact at various times throughout the history of language teaching, attempts have been made to make second language learning more like first language learning. In the sixteenth century, for example, Montaigne described how he was entrusted to a guardian who addressed him exclusively in Latin for the first years of his life, since Montaigne's father wanted his son to speak Latin well. Among those who tried to apply natural principles to language classes in the nineteenth century was L. Sauveur (1826–1907), who used intensive oral interaction in the target language, employing questions as a way of presenting and eliciting language. He opened a language school in Boston in the late 1860s, and his method soon became referred to as the Natural Method.

Sauveur and other believers in the Natural Method argued that a foreign language could be taught without translation or the use of the learner's native tongue if meaning was conveyed directly through demonstration and action. The German scholar F. Franke wrote on the psychological principles of direct association between forms and meanings in the target language (1884) and provided a theoretical justification for a monolingual approach to teaching. According to Franke, a language could best be taught by using it actively in the classroom. Rather than using analytical procedures that focus on explanation of grammar rules in classroom teaching, teachers must encourage direct and spontaneous use of the foreign language in the classroom. Learners would then be able to induce rules of grammar. The teacher replaced the textbook in the early stages of learning. Speaking began with systematic attention to pronunciation. Known words could be used to teach new vocabulary, using mime, demonstration, and pictures.

These natural language learning principles provided the foundation for what came to be known as the Direct Method, which refers to the most widely known of the natural methods. Enthusiastic supporters of the Direct Method introduced it in France and Germany (it was officially approved in both countries at the turn of the century), and it became widely known in the United States through its use by Sauveur and Maximilian Berlitz in successful commercial language schools. (Berlitz, in fact, never used the term; he referred to the method used in his schools as the Berlitz Method.) In practice it stood for the following principles and procedures:

1. Classroom instruction was conducted exclusively in the target language.
2. Only everyday vocabulary and sentences were taught.

3. Oral communication skills were built up in a carefully graded progression organized around question-and-answer exchanges between teachers and students in small, intensive classes.
4. Grammar was taught inductively.
5. New teaching points were introduced orally.
6. Concrete vocabulary was taught through demonstration, objects, and pictures; abstract vocabulary was taught by association of ideas.
7. Both speech and listening comprehension were taught.
8. Correct pronunciation and grammar were emphasized.

These principles are seen in the following guidelines for teaching oral language, which are still followed in contemporary Berlitz schools:

Never translate: demonstrate
Never explain: act
Never make a speech: ask questions
Never imitate mistakes: correct
Never speak with single words: use sentences
Never speak too much: make students speak much
Never use the book: use your lesson plan
Never jump around: follow your plan
Never go too fast: keep the pace of the student
Never speak too slowly: speak normally
Never speak too quickly: speak naturally
Never speak too loudly: speak naturally
Never be impatient: take it easy

(cited in Titone 1968:100–1)

The Direct Method was quite successful in private language schools, such as those of the Berlitz chain, where paying clients had high motivation and the use of native-speaking teachers was the norm. But despite pressure from proponents of the method, it was difficult to implement in public secondary school education. It overemphasized and distorted the similarities between naturalistic first language learning and classroom foreign language learning and failed to consider the practical realities of the classroom. In addition, it lacked a rigorous basis in applied linguistic theory, and for this reason it was often criticized by the more academically based proponents of the Reform Movement. The Direct Method represented the product of enlightened amateurism. It was perceived to have several drawbacks. First, it required teachers who were native speakers or who had nativelike fluency in the foreign language. It was largely dependent on the teacher's skill, rather than on a textbook, and not all teachers were proficient enough in the foreign language to adhere to the principles of the method. Critics pointed out that strict adherence to Direct Method principles was often counterproductive, since teachers were required to go to great lengths to avoid using the native tongue, when sometimes a simple brief explanation in the student's native tongue would have been a more efficient route to comprehension.

The Harvard psychologist Roger Brown has documented similar problems with strict Direct Method techniques. He described his frustration in observing a teacher performing verbal gymnastics in an attempt to convey the meaning of Japanese words, when translation would have been a much more efficient technique to use (Brown 1973: 5).

By the 1920s, use of the Direct Method in noncommercial schools in Europe had consequently declined. In France and Germany it was gradually modified into versions that combined some Direct Method techniques with more controlled grammar-based activities. The European popularity of the Direct Method in the early part of the twentieth century caused foreign language specialists in the United States to attempt to have it implemented in American schools and colleges, although they decided to move with caution. A study begun in 1923 on the state of foreign language teaching concluded that no single method could guarantee successful results. The goal of trying to teach conversation skills was considered impractical in view of the restricted time available for foreign language teaching in schools, the limited skills of teachers, and the perceived irrelevance of conversation skills in a foreign language for the average American college student. The study – published as the Coleman Report – advocated that a more reasonable goal for a foreign language course would be a reading knowledge of a foreign language, achieved through the gradual introduction of words and grammatical structures in simple reading texts. The main result of this recommendation was that reading became the goal of most foreign language programs in the United States (Coleman 1929). The emphasis on reading continued to characterize foreign language teaching in the United States until World War II.

Although the Direct Method enjoyed popularity in Europe, not everyone had embraced it enthusiastically. The British applied linguist Henry Sweet had recognized its limitations. It offered innovations at the level of teaching procedures but lacked a thorough methodological basis. Its main focus was on the exclusive use of the target language in the classroom, but it failed to address many issues that Sweet thought more basic. Sweet and other applied linguists argued for the development of sound methodological principles that could serve as the basis for teaching techniques. In the 1920s and 1930s applied linguists systematized the principles proposed earlier by the Reform Movement and so laid the foundations for what developed into the British approach to teaching English as a foreign language. Subsequent developments led to Audiolingualism (see Chapter 4) in the United States and the Oral Approach or Situational Language Teaching (see Chapter 3) in Britain.

What became of the concept of *method* as foreign language teaching emerged as a significant educational issue in the nineteenth and twentieth centuries? We have seen from this historical survey some of the questions that prompted innovations and new directions in language teaching in the past:

1. What should the goals of language teaching be? Should a language course try to teach conversational proficiency, reading, translation, or some other skill?
2. What is the basic nature of language, and how will this affect teaching method?
3. What are the principles for the selection of language content in language teaching?
4. What principles of organization, sequencing, and presentation best facilitate learning?
5. What should the role of the native language be?
6. What processes do learners use in mastering a language, and can these be incorporated into a method?
7. What teaching techniques and activities work best and under what circumstances?

Particular methods differ in the way they address these issues. But in order to understand the fundamental nature of methods in language teaching, it is necessary to conceive the notion of method more systematically. This is the aim of the next chapter, in which we present a model for the description, analysis, and comparison of methods. This model will be used as a framework for our subsequent discussions and analyses of particular language teaching methods and philosophies.

Bibliography

Brown, R. 1973. *A First Language*. Cambridge, Mass.: Harvard University Press.
Coleman, A. 1929. *The Teaching of Modern Foreign Languages in the United States*. New York: Macmillan.
Darian, Steven. 1972. *English as a Foreign Language: History, Development, and Methods of Teaching*. Norman: University of Oklahoma Press.
Diller, K. C. 1971. *Generative Grammar, Structural Linguistics, and Language Teaching*. Rowley, Mass.: Newbury House.
Franke, F. 1884. *Die praktische Spracherlernung auf Grund der Psychologie und der Physiologie der Sprache dargestellt*. Leipzig: O. R. Reisland.
Howatt, A. P. R. 1984. *A History of English Language Teaching*. Oxford: Oxford University Press.
Kelly, L. G. 1969. *25 Centuries of Language Teaching*. Rowley, Mass.: Newbury House.
Mackey, W. F. 1965. *Language Teaching Analysis*. London: Longman.
Stern, H. H. 1983. *Fundamental Concepts of Language Teaching*. Oxford: Oxford University Press.

Sweet, H. 1899. *The Practical Study of Languages*. Reprinted. London: Oxford University Press.

Titone, R. 1968. *Teaching Foreign Languages: An Historical Sketch*. Washington, D.C.: Georgetown University Press.

2 The nature of approaches and methods in language teaching

We saw in the preceding chapter that the changing rationale for foreign language study and the classroom techniques and procedures used to teach languages have reflected responses to a variety of historical issues and circumstances. Tradition was for many years the guiding principle. The Grammar-Translation Method reflected a time-honored and scholarly view of language and language study. At times, the practical realities of the classroom determined both goals and procedures, as with the determination of reading as the goal in American schools and colleges in the late 1920s. At other times, theories derived from linguistics, psychology, or a mixture of both were used to develop a both philosophical and practical basis for language teaching, as with the various reformist proposals of the nineteenth century. As the study of teaching methods and procedures in language teaching assumed a more central role within applied linguistics from the 1940s on, various attempts have been made to conceptualize the nature of methods and to explore more systematically the relationship between theory and practice within a method. In this chapter we will clarify the relationship between approach and method and present a model for the description, analysis, and comparison of methods.

Approach and method

When linguists and language specialists sought to improve the quality of language teaching in the late nineteenth century, they often did so by referring to general principles and theories concerning how languages are learned, how knowledge of language is represented and organized in memory, or how language itself is structured. The early applied linguists, such as Henry Sweet (1845–1912), Otto Jespersen (1860–1943), and Harold Palmer (1877–1949) (see Chapter 3), elaborated principles and theoretically accountable approaches to the design of language teaching programs, courses, and materials, though many of the specific practical details were left to be worked out by others. They sought a rational answer to questions, such as those regarding principles for the selection and sequencing of vocabulary and grammar, though none of these applied linguists saw in any existing method the ideal embodiment of their ideas.

In describing methods, the difference between a philosophy of language teaching at the level of theory and principles, and a set of derived procedures for teaching a language, is central. In an attempt to clarify this difference, a scheme was proposed by the American applied linguist Edward Anthony in 1963. He identified three levels of conceptualization and organization, which he termed *approach, method,* and *technique.*

The arrangement is hierarchical. The organizational key is that techniques carry out a method which is consistent with an approach...

...An approach is a set of correlative assumptions dealing with the nature of language teaching and learning. An approach is axiomatic. It describes the nature of the subject matter to be taught...

...Method is an overall plan for the orderly presentation of language material, no part of which contradicts, and all of which is based upon, the selected approach. An approach is axiomatic, a method is procedural.

Within one approach, there can be many methods...

...A technique is implementational – that which actually takes place in a classroom. It is a particular trick, strategem, or contrivance used to accomplish an immediate objective. Techniques must be consistent with a method, and therefore in harmony with an approach as well. (Anthony 1963:63–7)

According to Anthony's model, approach is the level at which assumptions and beliefs about language and language learning are specified; method is the level at which theory is put into practice and at which choices are made about the particular skills to be taught, the content to be taught, and the order in which the content will be presented; technique is the level at which classroom procedures are described.

Anthony's model serves as a useful way of distinguishing between different degrees of abstraction and specificity found in different language teaching proposals. Thus we can see that the proposals of the Reform Movement were at the level of approach and that the Direct Method is one method derived from this approach. The so-called Reading Method, which evolved as a result of the Coleman Report (see Chapter 1) should really be described in the plural – reading methods – since a number of different ways of implementing a reading approach have been developed.

A number of other ways of conceptualizing approaches and methods in language teaching have been proposed. Mackey, in his book *Language Teaching Analysis* (1965), elaborated perhaps the most well-known model of the 1960s, one that focuses primarily on the levels of method and technique. Mackey's model of language teaching analysis concentrates on the dimensions of selection, gradation, presentation, and repetition underlying a method. In fact, despite the title of Mackey's book, his concern is primarily with the analysis of textbooks and their underlying principles of organization. His model fails to address the level of approach, nor does it deal with the actual classroom behaviors of teachers and learners, except as these are represented in textbooks. Hence it cannot really serve as a basis for comprehensive analysis of either approaches or methods.

Although Anthony's original proposal has the advantage of simplicity and comprehensiveness and serves as a useful way of distinguishing the relationship between underlying theoretical principles and the practices derived from them, it fails to give sufficient attention to the nature of a method itself. Nothing is said about the roles of teachers and learners assumed in a method, for example, nor about the role of instructional materials or the form they are expected to take. It fails to account for how an approach may be realized in a method, or for how method and technique are related. In order to provide a more comprehensive model for the discussion and analysis of approaches and methods, we have revised and extended the original Anthony model. The primary areas needing further clarification are, using Anthony's terms, method and technique. We see approach and method treated at the level of design, that level in which objectives, syllabus, and content are determined, and in which the roles of teachers, learners, and instructional materials are specified. The implementation phase (the level of technique in Anthony's model) we refer to by the slightly more comprehensive term *procedure*. Thus, a method is theoretically related to an approach, is organizationally determined by a design, and is practically realized in procedure. In the remainder of this chapter we will elaborate on the relationship between approach, design, and procedure, using this framework to compare particular methods and approaches in language teaching. In the remaining chapters of the book we will use the model presented here as a basis for describing a number of widely used approaches and methods.

Approach

Following Anthony, *approach* refers to theories about the nature of language and language learning that serve as the source of practices and principles in language teaching. We will examine the linguistic and psycholinguistic aspects of approach in turn.

Theory of language

At least three different theoretical views of language and the nature of language proficiency explicitly or implicitly inform current approaches and methods in language teaching. The first, and the most traditional of the three, is the *structural view,* the view that language is a system of structurally related elements for the coding of meaning. The target of language learning is seen to be the mastery of elements of this system, which are generally defined in terms of phonological units (e.g., phonemes), grammatical units (e.g., clauses, phrases, sentences), grammatical operations (e.g., adding, shifting, joining, or transforming elements), and lexical items (e.g., function words and structure words). As we see in Chapter 4, the Audiolingual Method embodies this particular view of language, as do such contemporary methods as Total Physical Response (Chapter 6) and the Silent Way (Chapter 7).

The second view of language is the *functional view,* the view that language is a vehicle for the expression of functional meaning. The communicative movement in language teaching subscribes to this view of language (see Chapter 9). This theory emphasizes the semantic and communicative dimension rather than merely the grammatical characteristics of language, and leads to a specification and organization of language teaching content by categories of meaning and function rather than by elements of structure and grammar. Wilkins's *Notional Syllabuses* (1976) is an attempt to spell out the implications of this view of language for syllabus design. A notional syllabus would include not only elements of grammar and lexis but also specify the topics, notions, and concepts the learner needs to communicate about. The English for specific purposes (ESP) movement likewise begins not from a structural theory of language but from a functional account of learner needs (Robinson 1980.)

The third view of language can be called the *interactional view.* It sees language as a vehicle for the realization of interpersonal relations and for the performance of social transactions between individuals. Language is seen as a tool for the creation and maintenance of social relations. Areas of inquiry being drawn on in the development of interactional approaches to language teaching include interaction analysis, conversation analysis, and ethnomethodology. Interactional theories focus on the patterns of moves, acts, negotiation, and interaction found in conversational exchanges. Language teaching content, according to this view, may be specified and organized by patterns of exchange and interaction or may be left unspecified, to be shaped by the inclinations of learners as interactors.

Structural, functional, or interactional models of language (or variations on them) provide the axioms and theoretical framework that may motivate a particular teaching method, such as Audiolingualism. But in themselves they are incomplete and need to be complemented by theories of language learning. It is to this dimension that we now turn.

Theory of language learning

Although specific theories of the nature of language may provide the basis for a particular teaching method, other methods derive primarily from a theory of language learning. A learning theory underlying an approach or method responds to two questions: (a) What are the psycholinguistic and cognitive processes involved in language learning? and (b) What are the conditions that need to be met in order for these learning processes to be activated? Learning theories associated with a method at the level of approach may emphasize either one or both of these dimensions. Process-oriented theories build on learning processes, such as habit formation, induction, inferencing, hypothesis testing, and generalization. Condition-oriented theories emphasize the nature of the human and physical context in which language learning takes place.

Stephen D. Krashen's Monitor Model of second language development (1981) is an example of a learning theory on which a method (the Natural Approach) has been built (see Chapter 9). Monitor theory addresses both the process and the condition dimensions of learning. At the level of process, Krashen distinguishes between acquisition and learning. *Acquisition* refers to the natural assimilation of language rules through using language for communication. *Learning* refers to the formal study of language rules and is a conscious process. According to Krashen, however, learning is available only as a "monitor." The monitor is the repository of conscious grammatical knowledge about a language that is learned through formal instruction and that is called upon in the editing of utterances produced through the acquired system. Krashen's theory also addresses the conditions necessary for the process of "acquisition" to take place. Krashen describes these in terms of the type of "input" the learner receives. Input must be comprehensible, slightly above the learner's present level of competence, interesting or relevant, not grammatically sequenced, in sufficient quantity, and experienced in low-anxiety contexts.

Tracy D. Terrell's Natural Approach (1977) is an example of a method derived primarily from a learning theory rather than from a particular view of language. Although the Natural Approach is based on a learning theory that specifies both processes and conditions, the learning theory underlying such methods as Counseling-Learning and the Silent Way addresses primarily the conditions held to be necessary for learning to take place without specifying what the learning processes themselves are presumed to be (see Chapters 7 and 8).

Charles A. Curran in his writings on Counseling-Learning (1972), for example, focuses primarily on the conditions necessary for successful learning. He believes the atmosphere of the classroom is a crucial factor, and his method seeks to ameliorate the feelings of intimidation and insecurity that many learners experience. James Asher's Total Physical Response (Asher 1977) is likewise a method that derives primarily from learning theory rather than from a theory of the nature of language (see Chapter 6). Asher's learning theory addresses both the process and condition aspects of learning. It is based on the belief that child language learning is based on motor activity, on coordinating language with action, and that this should form the basis of adult foreign language teaching. Orchestrating language production and comprehension with body movement and physical actions is thought to provide the conditions for success in language learning. Caleb Gattegno's Silent Way (1972, 1976) is likewise built around a theory of the conditions necessary for successful learning to be realized. Gattegno's writings address learners' needs to feel secure about learning and to assume conscious control of learning. Many of the techniques used in the method are designed to train learners to consciously use their intelligence to heighten learning potential.

There often appear to be natural affinities between certain theories of language and theories of language learning; however, one can imagine different pairings of language theory and learning theory that might work as well as those we observe. The linking of structuralism (a linguistic theory) to behaviorism (a learning theory) produced Audiolingualism. That particular link was not inevitable, however. Cognitive-code proponents (see Chapter 4), for example, have attempted to link a more sophisticated model of structuralism to a more mentalistic and less behavioristic brand of learning theory.

At the level of approach, we are hence concerned with theoretical principles. With respect to language theory, we are concerned with a model of language competence and an account of the basic features of linguistic organization and language use. With respect to learning theory, we are concerned with an account of the central processes of learning and an account of the conditions believed to promote successful language learning. These principles may or may not lead to "a" method. Teachers may, for example, develop their own teaching procedures, informed by a particular view of language and a particular theory of learning. They may constantly revise, vary, and modify teaching/learning procedures on the basis of the performance of the learners and their reactions to instructional practice. A group of teachers holding similar beliefs about language and language learning (i.e., sharing a similar approach) may each implement these principles in different ways. Approach does not specify procedure. Theory does not dictate a particular set of teaching techniques and activities. What links theory with practice (or approach with procedure) is what we have called design.

Design

In order for an approach to lead to a method, it is necessary to develop a design for an instructional system. *Design* is the level of method analysis in which we consider (a) what the objectives of a method are; (b) how language content is selected and organized within the method, that is, the syllabus model the method incorporates; (c) the types of learning tasks and teaching activities the method advocates; (d) the roles of learners; (e) the roles of teachers; (f) the role of instructional materials.

Objectives

Different theories of language and language learning influence the focus of a method; that is, they determine what a method sets out to achieve. The specification of particular learning objectives, however, is a product of design, not of approach. Some methods focus primarily on oral skills and say that reading and writing skills are secondary and derive from transfer of oral skills. Some methods set out to teach general communication skills and give greater priority to the ability to express oneself meaningfully and to make oneself understood than to grammatical accuracy or perfect pronunciation. Others place a greater emphasis on accurate grammar and pronunciation from the very beginning. Some methods set out to teach the basic grammar and vocabulary of a language. Others may define their objectives less in linguistic terms than in terms of learning behaviors, that is, in terms of the processes or abilities the learner is expected to acquire as a result of instruction. Gattegno writes, for example, "Learning is not seen as the means of accumulating knowledge but as the means of becoming a more proficient learner in whatever one is engaged in" (1972:89). This process-oriented objective may be offered in contrast to the linguistically oriented or product-oriented objectives of more traditional methods. The degree to which a method has process-oriented or product-oriented objectives may be revealed in how much emphasis is placed on vocabulary acquisition and grammatical proficiency and in how grammatical or pronunciation errors are treated in the method. Many methods that claim to be primarily process oriented in fact show overriding concerns with grammatical and lexical attainment and with accurate grammar and pronunciation.

Content choice and organization: the syllabus

All methods of language teaching involve the use of the target language. All methods thus involve overt or covert decisions concerning the selection of language items (words, sentence patterns, tenses, constructions, functions, topics, etc.) that are to be used within a course or method. Decisions about the choice of language content relate both to subject matter and linguistic matter. In straightforward terms, one makes decisions about what to talk about (subject matter) and how to talk about it (linguistic matter). ESP courses, for example, are necessarily subject-matter focused. Structurally based methods, such as Situational Language Teaching and the Audiolingual Method, are necessarily linguistically focused. Methods typically differ in what they see as the relevant language and subject matter around which language teaching should be organized and the principles used in sequencing content within a course. Content issues involve the principles of selection (Mackey 1965) that ultimately shape the syllabus adopted in a course as well as the instructional materials that are used, together with the principles of gradation the method adopts. In grammar-based courses matters of sequencing and gradation are generally determined according to the difficulty of items or their frequency. In communicative or functionally oriented courses (e.g., in ESP programs) sequencing may be according to the learners' communicative needs.

Traditionally the term *syllabus* has been used to refer to the form in which linguistic content is specified in a course or method. Inevitably the term has been more closely associated with methods that are product centered rather than those that are process centered. Syllabuses and syllabus principles for Audiolingual, Structural-Situational, and notional-functional methods as well as in ESP approaches to language program design can be readily identified. The syllabus underlying the Situational and Audiolingual methods consists of a list of grammatical items and constructions, often together with an associated list of vocabulary items (Fries and Fries 1961; Alexander et al. 1975). Notional-functional syllabuses specify the communicative content of a course in terms of functions, notions, topics, grammar, and vocabulary. Such syllabuses are usually determined in advance of teaching and for this reason have been referred to as "a priori syllabuses."

The term *syllabus*, however, is less frequently used in process-based methods, in which considerations of language content are often secondary. Counseling-Learning, for example, has no language syllabus as such. Neither linguistic matter nor subject matter is specified in advance. Learners select content for themselves by choosing topics they want to talk about. These are then translated into the target language and used as the basis for interaction and language practice. To find out what linguistic content had in fact been generated and practiced during a course organized according to Counseling-Learning principles, it would be necessary to record the lessons and later determine what items of language had been covered. This would be an a posteriori approach to syllabus specification; that is, the syllabus would be determined from examining lesson protocols. With such methods as the Silent Way and Total Physical Response, an examination of lesson protocols, teacher's manuals, and texts derived from them reveals that the syllabuses underlying these methods are traditional lexico-grammatical syllabuses. In both there is a strong emphasis on grammar and grammatical accuracy.

Types of learning and teaching activities

The objectives of a method, whether defined primarily in terms of product or process, are attained through the instructional process, through the organized and directed interaction of teachers, learners, and materials in the classroom. Differences among methods at the level of approach manifest themselves in the choice of different kinds of learning and teaching activities in the classroom. Teaching activities that focus on grammatical accuracy may be quite different from those that focus on communicative skills. Activities designed to focus on the development of specific psycholinguistic processes in language acquisition will differ from those directed toward mastery of particular features of grammar. The activity types that a method advocates – the third component in the level of design in method analysis – often serve to distinguish methods. Audiolingualism, for example, uses dialogue and pattern practice extensively. The Silent Way employs problem-solving activities that involve the use of special charts and colored rods. Communicative language teaching theoreticians have advocated the use of tasks that involve an "information gap" and "information transfer"; that is, learners work on the same task, but each learner has different information needed to complete the task.

Different philosophies at the level of approach may be reflected both in the use of different kinds of activities and in different uses for particular activity types. For example, interactive games are often used in audiolingual courses for motivation and to provide a change of pace from pattern-practice drills. In communicative language teaching the same games may be used to introduce or provide practice for particular types of interactive exchanges. Differences in activity types in methods may also involve different arrangements and groupings of learners. A method that stresses oral chorus drilling will require different groupings of learners in the classroom from a method that uses problem-solving/ information-exchange activities involving pair work. Activity types in methods thus include the primary categories of learning and teaching activity the method advocates, such as dialogue, responding to commands, group problem solving, information-exchange activities, improvisations, question and answer, or drills.

Because of the different assumptions they make about learning processes, syllabuses, and learning activities, methods also attribute different roles and functions to teachers, learners, and instructional materials within the instructional process. These constitute the next three components of design in method analysis.

Learner roles

The design of an instructional system will be considerably influenced by how learners are regarded. A method reflects explicit or implicit responses to questions concerning the learners' contribution to the learning process. This is seen in the types of activities learners carry out, the degree of control learners have over the content of learning, the patterns of learner groupings adopted, the degree to which learners influence the learning of others, and the view of the learner as processor, performer, initiator, problem solver.

Much of the criticism of Audiolingualism came from the recognition of the very limited roles available to learners in audiolingual methodology. Learners were seen as stimulus-response mechanisms whose learning was a direct result of repetitive practice. Newer methodologies customarily exhibit more concern for learner roles and for variation among learners. Johnson and Paulston (1976) spell out learner roles in an individualized approach to language learning in the following terms: (a) Learners plan their own learning program and thus ultimately assume responsibility for what they do in the classroom. (b) Learners monitor and evaluate their own progress. (c) Learners are members of a group and learn by interacting with others. (d) Learners tutor other learners. (e) Learners learn from the teacher, from other students, and from other teaching sources. Counseling-Learning views learners as having roles that change developmentally, and Curran (1976) uses an ontogenetic metaphor to suggest this development. He divides the developmental process into five stages, extending from total dependency on the teacher in stage 1 to total independence in stage 5. These learner stages Curran sees as parallel to the growth of a child from embryo to independent adulthood passing through childhood and adolescence.

Teacher roles

Learner roles in an instructional system are closely linked to the teacher's status and function. Teacher roles are similarly related ultimately both to assumptions about language and language learning at the level of approach. Some methods are totally dependent on the teacher as a source of knowledge and direction; others see the teacher's role as catalyst, consultant, guide, and model for learning; still others try to "teacher-proof" the instructional system by limiting teacher initiative and by building instructional content and direction into texts or lesson plans.

Teacher and learner roles define the type of interaction characteristic of classrooms in which a particular method is being used.

Teacher roles in methods are related to the following issues: (a) the types of functions teachers are expected to fulfill, whether that of practice director, counselor, or model, for example; (b) the degree of control the teacher has over how learning takes place; (c) the degree to which the teacher is responsible for determining the content of what is taught; and (d) the interactional patterns that develop between teachers and learners. Methods typically depend critically on teacher roles and their realizations. In the classical Audiolingual Method, the teacher is regarded as the primary source of language and of language learning. But less teacher-directed learning may still demand very specific and sometimes even more demanding roles for the teacher. The role of the teacher in the Silent Way, for example, depends upon thorough training and methodological initiation. Only teachers who are thoroughly sure of their role and the concomitant learner's role will risk departure from the security of traditional textbook-oriented teaching.

For some methods, the role of the teacher has been specified in detail. Individualized approaches to learning define roles for the teacher that create specific patterns of interaction between teachers and learners in classrooms. These are designed to shift the responsibility for learning gradually from the teacher to the learner. Counseling-Learning sees the teacher's role as that of psychological counselor, the effectiveness of the teacher's role being a measure of counseling skills and attributes — warmth, sensitivity, and acceptance.

As these examples suggest, the potential role relationships of learner and teacher are many and varied. They may be asymmetrical relationships, such as those of conductor to orchestra member, therapist to patient, coach to player. Some contemporary methodologies have sought to establish more symmetrical kinds of learner–teacher relationships, such as friend to friend, colleague to colleague, teammate to teammate. The role of the teacher will ultimately reflect both the objectives of the method and the learning theory on which the method is predicated, since the success of a method may depend on the degree to which the teacher can provide the content or create the conditions for successful language learning.

The role of instructional materials

The last component within the level of design concerns the role of instructional materials within the instructional system. What is specified with respect to objectives, content (i.e., the syllabus), learning activities, and learner and teacher roles suggests the function for materials within the system. The syllabus defines linguistic content in terms of language elements – structures, topics, notions, functions – or in some cases in terms of learning tasks (see Johnson 1982; Prabhu 1983). It also defines the goals for language learning in terms of speaking, listening, reading, or writing skills. The instructional materials in their turn further specify subject matter content, even where no syllabus exists, and define or suggest the intensity of coverage for syllabus items, allocating the amount of time, attention, and detail particular syllabus items or tasks require. Instructional materials also define or imply the day-to-day learning objectives that collectively constitute the goals of the syllabus. Materials designed on the assumption that learning is initiated and monitored by the teacher must meet quite different requirements from those designed for student self-instruction or for peer tutoring. Some methods require the instructional use of existing materials, found materials, and realia. Some assume teacher-proof materials that even poorly trained teachers with imperfect control of the target language can teach with. Some materials require specially trained teachers with near-native competence in the target language. Some are designed to replace the teacher, so that learning can take place independently. Some materials dictate various interactional patterns in the classroom; others inhibit classroom interaction; still others are noncommittal about interaction between teacher and learner and learner and learner.

The role of instructional materials within a method or instructional system will reflect decisions concerning the primary goal of materials (e.g., to present content, to practice content, to facilitate communication between learners, or to enable learners to practice content without the teacher's help), the form of materials (e.g., textbook, audiovisuals, computer software), the relation of materials to other sources of input (i.e., whether they serve as the major source of input or only as a minor component of it), and the abilities of teachers (e.g., their competence in the language or degree of training and experience.)

A particular design for an instructional system may imply a particular set of roles for materials in support of the syllabus and the teachers and learners. For example, the role of instructional materials within a functional/communicative methodology might be specified in the following terms:

1. Materials will focus on the communicative abilities of interpretation, expression, and negotiation.
2. Materials will focus on understandable, relevant, and interesting exchanges of information, rather than on the presentation of grammatical form.
3. Materials will involve different kinds of texts and different media, which the learners can use to develop their competence through a variety of different activities and tasks.

By comparison, the role of instructional materials within an individualized instructional system might include the following specifications:

1. Materials will allow learners to progress at their own rates of learning.
2. Materials will allow for different styles of learning.
3. Materials will provide opportunities for independent study and use.
4. Materials will provide opportunities for self-evaluation and progress in learning.

The content of a method such as Counseling-Learning is assumed to be a product of the interests of the learners, since learners generate their own subject matter. In that sense it would appear that no linguistic content or materials are specified within the method. On the other hand, Counseling-Learning acknowledges the need for learner mastery of certain linguistic mechanics, such as the mastery of vocabulary, grammar, and pronunciation. Counseling-Learning sees these issues as falling outside the teacher's central role as counselor. Thus Counseling-Learning has proposed the use of teaching machines and other programmed materials to support the learning of some of the more mechanical aspects of language so as to free the teacher to function increasingly as a learning counselor.

Procedure

The last level of conceptualization and organization within a method is what we will refer to as *procedure*. This encompasses the actual moment-to-moment techniques, practices, and behaviors that operate in teaching a language according to a particular method. It is the level at which we describe how a method realizes its approach and design in classroom behavior. At the level of design we saw that a method will advocate the use of certain types of teaching activities as a consequence of its theoretical assumptions about language and learning. At the level of procedure we are concerned with how these tasks and activities are integrated into lessons and used as the basis for teaching and learning. There are three dimensions to a method at the level of procedure: (a) the use of teaching activities (drills, dialogues, information-gap activities, etc.) to present new language and to clarify and demonstrate formal, communicative, or other aspects of the target language; (b) the ways in which particular teaching activities are used for practicing language; and (c) the procedures and techniques used in giving feedback to learners concerning the form or content of their utterances or sentences.

Essentially, then, procedure focuses on the way a method handles the presentation, practice, and feedback phases of teaching. Here, for example, is a description of the procedural aspects of a beginning Silent Way course based on Stevick (1980: 44–5):

1. The teacher points at meaningless symbols on a wall chart. The symbols represent the syllables of the spoken language. The students read the sounds aloud, first in chorus and then individually.
2. After the students can pronounce the sounds, the teacher moves to a second set of charts containing words frequently used in the language, including numbers. The teacher leads the students to pronounce long numbers.
3. The teacher uses colored rods together with charts and gestures to lead the students into producing the words and basic grammatical structures needed.

Of error treatment in the Silent Way Stevick notes:

When the students respond correctly to the teacher's initiative, she usually does not react with any overt confirmation that what they did was right. If a student's response is wrong, on the other hand, she indicates that the student needs to do further work on the word or phrase; if she thinks it necessary, she actually shows the student exactly where the additional work is to be done. (1980: 45)

Finnocchiaro and Brumfit (1983) illustrate how the procedural phases of instruction are handled in what they call a notional-functional approach.

1. Presentation of a brief dialogue or several mini-dialogues.
2. Oral practice of each utterance in the dialogue.
3. Questions and answers based on the topic and situation in the dialogue.
4. Questions and answers related to the student's personal experience but centered on the theme of the dialogue.
5. Study of the basic communicative expressions used in the dialogue or one of the structures that exemplify the function.
6. Learner discovery of generalizations or rules underlying the functional expression of structure.
7. Oral recognition, interpretative procedures.
8. Oral production activities, proceeding from guided to freer communication.

We expect methods to be most obviously idiosyncratic at the level of procedure, though classroom observations often reveal that teachers do not necessarily follow the procedures a method prescribes (see Chapter 11).

The elements and subelements that constitute a method and that we have described under the rubrics of approach, design, and procedure are summarized in Figure 2.1.

Method

| Approach | Design | Procedure |

Approach

a. *A theory of the nature of language*
  – an account of the nature of language proficiency
  – an account of the basic units of language structure
b. *A theory of the nature of language learning*
  – an account of the psycholinguistic and cognitive processes involved in language learning
  – an account of the conditions that allow for successful use of these processes

Design

a. *The general and specific objectives of the method*
b. *A syllabus model*
  – criteria for the selection and organization of linguistic and/or subject-matter content
c. *Types of learning and teaching activities*
  – kinds of tasks and practice activities to be employed in the classroom and in materials
d. *Learner roles*
  – types of learning tasks set for learners
  – degree of control learners have over the content of learning
  – patterns of learner groupings that are recommended or implied
  – degree to which learners influence the learning of others
  – the view of the learner as a processor, performer, initiator, problem solver, etc.
e. *Teacher roles*
  – types of functions teachers fulfill
  – degree of teacher influence over learning
  – degree to which the teacher determines the content of learning
  – types of interaction between teachers and learners
f. *The role of instructional materials*
  – primary function of materials
  – the form materials take (e.g., textbook, audiovisual)
  – relation of materials to other input
  – assumptions made about teachers and learners

Procedure

a. *Classroom techniques, practices, and behaviors observed when the method is used*
  – resources in terms of time, space, and equipment used by the teacher
  – interactional patterns observed in lessons
  – tactics and strategies used by teachers and learners when the method is being used

Figure 2.1 Summary of elements and subelements that constitute a method

Conclusion

The model presented in this chapter demonstrates that any language teaching method can be described in terms of the issues identified here at the levels of approach, design, and procedure. Very few methods are explicit with respect to all of these dimensions, however. In the remaining chapters of this book we will attempt to make each of these features of approach, design, and procedure explicit with reference to the major language teaching approaches and methods in use today. In so doing, we will often have to infer from what method developers have written in order to determine precisely what criteria are being used for teaching activities, what claims are being made about learning theory, what type of syllabus is being employed, and so on.

The model presented here is not intended to imply that methodological development proceeds neatly from approach, through design, to procedure. It is not clear whether such a developmental formula is possible, and our model certainly does not describe the typical case. Methods can develop out of any of the three categories. One can, for example, stumble on or invent a set of teaching procedures that appear to be successful and then later develop a design and theoretical approach that explain or justify the procedures. Some methodologists would resist calling their proposals a method, although if descriptions are possible at each of the levels described here, we would argue that what is advocated has, in fact, the status of a method. Let us now turn to the major approaches and teaching methods that are in use today and examine them according to how they reflect specific decisions at the levels of approach, design, and procedure.

Bibliography

Alexander, L. G., W. S. Allen, R. A. Close, and R. J. O'Neill. 1975. *English Grammatical Structure*. London: Longman.

Anthony, E. M. 1963. Approach, method and technique. *English Language Teaching* 17: 63–7.

Asher, James J. 1977. *Learning Another Language Through Actions: The Complete Teacher's Guidebook*. Los Gatos, Cal.: Sky Oaks Productions.

Bosco, F. J., and R. J. Di Pietro. 1970. Instructional strategies: their psychological and linguistic bases. *International Review of Applied Linguistics* 8: 1–19.

Breen, M. P., and C. Candlin. 1980. The essentials of a communicative curriculum in language teaching. *Applied Linguistics* 1(2): 89–112.

Curran, C. A. 1972. *Counseling-Learning: A Whole-Person Model for Education*. New York: Grune and Stratton.

Curran, C. A. 1976. *Counseling-Learning in Second Languages*. Apple River, Ill.: Apple River Press.

Finocchiaro, M., and C. Brumfit. 1983. *The Functional-Notional Approach: From Theory to Practice*. New York: Oxford University Press.

Fries, C. C., and A. C. Fries. 1961. *Foundations for English Teaching*. Tokyo: Kenkyusha.

Gattegno, C. 1972. *Teaching Foreign Languages in Schools: The Silent Way*. 2nd ed. New York: Educational Solutions.

Gattegno, C. 1976. *The Common Sense of Teaching Foreign Languages*. New York: Educational Solutions.

Johnson, F., and C. B. Paulston. 1976. *Individualizing in the Language Classroom*. Cambridge, Mass.: Jacaranda.

Johnson, K. 1982. *Communicative Syllabus Design and Methodology*. Oxford: Pergamon.

Krashen, S. D. 1981. *Second Language Acquisition and Second Language Learning*. Oxford: Pergamon.

Mackey, W. F. 1965. *Language Teaching Analysis*. London: Longman.

Prahbu, N. 1983. Procedural syllabuses. Paper presented at the RELC Seminar, Singapore.

Robinson, P. 1980. *ESP (English for Specific Purposes)*. Oxford: Pergamon.

Stevick, E. W. 1980. *Teaching Languages: A Way and Ways*. Rowley, Mass.: Newbury House.

Terrell, T. D. 1977. A natural approach to the acquisition and learning of a language. *Modern Language Journal* 61(7): 325–36.

Wilkins, D. A. 1976. *Notional Syllabuses: A Taxonomy and Its Relevance to Foreign Language Curriculum Development*. Oxford: Oxford University Press.

3 The Oral Approach and Situational Language Teaching

Few language teachers in the 1980s are familiar with the terms *Oral Approach* or *Situational Language Teaching*, which refer to an approach to language teaching developed by British applied linguists from the 1930s to the 1960s. Even though neither term is commonly used today, the impact of the Oral Approach has been long lasting, and it has shaped the design of many widely used EFL/ESL textbooks and courses, including many still being used today. One of the most successful ESL courses of recent times, *Streamline English* (Hartley and Viney 1979), reflects the classic principles of Situational Language Teaching, as do many other widely used series (e.g., *Access to English*, Coles and Lord 1975; *Kernel Lessons Plus*, O'Neill 1973; and many of L. G. Alexander's widely used textbooks, e.g., Alexander 1967). As a recent British methodology text states, "This method is widely used at the time of writing and a very large number of textbooks are based on it" (Hubbard et al. 1983: 36). It is important therefore to understand the principles and practices of the Oral Approach and Situational Language Teaching.

Background

The origins of this approach began with the work of British applied linguists in the 1920s and 1930s. Beginning at this time, a number of outstanding applied linguists developed the basis for a principled approach to methodology in language teaching. Two of the leaders in this movement were Harold Palmer and A. S. Hornby, two of the most prominent figures in British twentieth-century language teaching. Both were familiar with the work of such linguists as Otto Jespersen and Daniel Jones, as well as with the Direct Method. What they attempted was to develop a more scientific foundation for an oral approach to teaching English than was evidenced in the Direct Method. The result was a systematic study of the principles and procedures that could be applied to the selection and organization of the content of a language course (Palmer 1917, 1921).

Vocabulary control

One of the first aspects of method design to receive attention was the role of vocabulary. In the 1920s and 1930s several large-scale investigations of foreign language vocabulary were undertaken. The impetus for this research came from two quarters. First, there was a general consensus among language teaching specialists, such as Palmer, that vocabulary was one of the most important aspects of foreign language learning. A second influence was the increased emphasis on reading skills as the goal of foreign language study in some countries. This had been the recommendation of the Coleman Report (Chapter 1) and also the independent conclusion of another British language teaching specialist, Michael West, who had examined the role of English in India in the 1920s. Vocabulary was seen as an essential component of reading proficiency.

This led to the development of principles of vocabulary control, which were to have a major practical impact on the teaching of English in the following decades. Frequency counts showed that a core of 2,000 or so words occurred frequently in written texts and that a knowledge of these words would greatly assist in reading a foreign language. Harold Palmer, Michael West, and other specialists produced a guide to the English vocabulary needed for teaching English as a foreign language, *The Interim Report on Vocabulary Selection* (Faucett et al. 1936), based on frequency as well as other criteria. This was later revised by West and published in 1953 as *A General Service List of English Words*, which became a standard reference in developing teaching materials. These efforts to introduce a scientific and rational basis for choosing the vocabulary content of a language course represented the first attempts to establish principles of syllabus design in language teaching.

Grammar control

Parallel to the interest in developing rational principles for vocabulary selection was a focus on the grammatical content of a language course. Palmer in his writings had emphasized the problems of grammar for the foreign learner. Much of his work in Japan, where he directed the Institute for Research in English Teaching from 1922 until World War II, was directed toward developing classroom procedures suited to teaching basic grammatical patterns through an oral approach. His view of grammar was very different from the abstract model of grammar seen in the Grammar-Translation Method, however, which was based on the assumption that one universal logic formed the basis of all languages and that the teacher's responsibility was to show how each category of the universal grammar was to be expressed in the foreign language. Palmer viewed grammar as the underlying sentence patterns of the spoken language. Palmer, Hornby, and other British applied linguists analyzed English and classified its major grammatical structures into sentence patterns (later called "substitution tables"), which could be used to help internalize the rules of English sentence structure.

A classification of English sentence patterns was incorporated into the first dictionary for students of English as a foreign language, developed by Hornby, Gatenby, and Wakefield and published in 1953 as *The Advanced Learner's Dictionary of Current English*. A number of pedagogically motivated descriptions of English grammar were undertaken including *A Grammar of Spoken English on a Strictly Phonetic Basis* (Palmer and Blandford 1939), *A Handbook of English Grammar* (Zandvoort 1945), and Hornby's *Guide to Patterns and Usage in English* (1954), which became a standard reference source of basic English sentence patterns for textbook writers. With the development of systematic approaches to the lexical and grammatical content of a language course and with the efforts of such specialists as Palmer, West, and Hornby in using these resources as part of a comprehensive methodological framework for the teaching of English as a foreign language, the foundations for the British approach in TEFL/TESL – the Oral Approach – were firmly established.

The Oral Approach and Situational Language Teaching

Palmer, Hornby, and other British applied linguists from the 1920s onward developed an approach to methodology that involved systematic principles of *selection* (the procedures by which lexical and grammatical content was chosen), *gradation* (principles by which the organization and sequencing of content were determined), and *presentation* (techniques used for presentation and practice of items in a course). Although Palmer, Hornby, and other English teaching specialists had differing views on the specific procedures to be used in teaching English, their general principles were referred to as the Oral Approach to language teaching. This was not to be confused with the Direct Method, which, although it used oral procedures, lacked a systematic basis in applied linguistic theory and practice.

An oral approach should not be confused with the obsolete Direct Method, which meant only that the learner was bewildered by a flow of ungraded speech, suffering all the difficulties he would have encountered in picking up the language in its normal environment and losing most of the compensating

33

benefits of better contextualization in those circumstances. (Patterson 1964: 4)

The Oral Approach was the accepted British approach to English language teaching by the 1950s. It is described in the standard methodology textbooks of the period, such as French (1948–50), Gurrey (1955), Frisby (1957), and Billows (1961). Its principles are seen in Hornby's famous *Oxford Progressive English Course for Adult Learners* (1954–6) and in many other more recent textbooks. One of the most active proponents of the Oral Approach in the sixties was the Australian George Pittman. Pittman and his colleagues were responsible for developing an influential set of teaching materials based on the situational approach, which were widely used in Australia, New Guinea, and the Pacific territories. Most Pacific territories continue to use the so-called Tate materials, developed by Pittman's colleague Gloria Tate. Pittman was also responsible for the situationally based materials developed by the Commonwealth Office of Education in Sydney, Australia, used in the English programs for immigrants in Australia. These were published for worldwide use in 1965 as the series *Situational English*. Materials by Alexander and other leading British textbook writers also reflected the principles of Situational Language Teaching as they had evolved over a twenty-year period. The main characteristics of the approach were as follows:

1. Language teaching begins with the spoken language. Material is taught orally before it is presented in written form.
2. The target language is the language of the classroom.
3. New language points are introduced and practiced situationally.
4. Vocabulary selection procedures are followed to ensure that an essential general service vocabulary is covered.
5. Items of grammar are graded following the principle that simple forms should be taught before complex ones.
6. Reading and writing are introduced once a sufficient lexical and grammatical basis is established.

It was the third principle that became a key feature of the approach in the sixties, and it was then that the term *situational* was used increasingly in referring to the Oral Approach. Hornby himself used the term *the Situational Approach* in the title of an influential series of articles published in *English Language Teaching* in 1950. Later the terms *Structural-Situational Approach* and *Situational Language Teaching* came into common usage. To avoid further confusion we will use the term *Situational Language Teaching* (SLT) to include the Structural-Situational and Oral approaches. How can Situational Language Teaching be characterized at the levels of approach, design, and procedure?

Approach

Theory of language

The theory of language underlying Situational Language Teaching can be characterized as a type of British "structuralism." Speech was regarded as the basis of language, and structure was viewed as being at the heart of speaking ability. Palmer, Hornby, and other British applied linguists had prepared pedagogical descriptions of the basic grammatical structures of English, and these were to be followed in developing methodology. "Word order, Structural Words, the few inflexions of English, and Content Words, will form the material of our teaching" (Frisby 1957: 134). In terms of language theory, there was little to distinguish such a view from that proposed by American linguists, such as Charles Fries. Indeed, Pittman drew heavily on Fries's theories of language in the sixties, but American theory was largely unknown by British applied linguists in the fifties. The British theoreticians, however, had a different focus to their version of structuralism – the notion of "situation." "Our principal classroom activity in the teaching of English structure will be the oral practice of structures. This oral practice of controlled sentence patterns should be given in situations designed to give the greatest amount of practice in English speech to the pupil" (Pittman 1963: 179).

The theory that knowledge of structures must be linked to situations in which they could be used gave Situational Language Teaching one of its distinctive features. This may have reflected the functional trend in British linguistics since the thirties. Many British linguists had emphasized the close relationship between the structure of language and the context and situations in which language is used. British linguists, such as J. R. Firth and M. A. K. Halliday, developed powerful views of language in which meaning, context, and situation were given a prominent place: "The emphasis now is on the description of language activity as part of the whole complex of events which, together with the participants and relevant objects, make up actual situations" (Halliday, McIntosh, and Strevens 1964: 38). Thus, in contrast to American structuralist views on language (see Chapter 4), language was viewed as purposeful activity related to goals and situations in the real world. "The language which a person originates . . . is always expressed for a purpose" (Frisby 1957: 16).

Theory of learning

The theory of learning underlying Situational Language Teaching is a type of behaviorist habit-learning theory. It addresses primarily the processes rather than the conditions of learning. Frisby, for example, cites Palmer's views as authoritative:

As Palmer has pointed out, there are three processes in learning a language – receiving the knowledge or materials, fixing it in the memory by repetition, and using it in actual practice until it becomes a personal skill. (1957: 136)

French likewise saw language learning as habit formation.

The fundamental is correct speech habits. . . . The pupils should be able to put the words, without hesitation and almost without thought, into sentence patterns which are correct. Such speech habits can be cultivated by blind imitative drill. (1950, vol. 3: 9)

Like the Direct Method, Situational Language Teaching adopts an inductive approach to the teaching of grammar. The meaning of words or structures is not to be given through explanation in either the native tongue or the target language but is to be induced from the way the form is used in a situation. "If we give the meaning of a new word, either by translation into the home language or by an equivalent in the same language, as soon as we introduce it, we weaken the impression which the word makes on the mind" (Billows 1961: 28). Explanation is therefore discouraged, and the learner is expected to deduce the meaning of a particular structure or vocabulary item from the situation in which it is presented. Extending structures and vocabulary to new situations takes place by generalization. The learner is expected to apply the language learned in a classroom to situations outside the classroom. This is how child language learning is believed to take place, and the same processes are thought to occur in second and foreign language learning, according to practitioners of Situational Language Teaching.

Design

Objectives

The objectives of the Situational Language Teaching method are to teach a practical command of the four basic skills of language, goals it shares with most methods of language teaching. But the skills are approached through structure. Accuracy in both pronunciation and grammar is regarded as crucial, and errors are to be avoided at all costs. Automatic control of basic structures and sentence patterns is fundamental to reading and writing skills, and this is achieved through speech work. "Before our pupils read new structures and new vocabulary, we shall teach orally both the new structures and the new vocabulary" (Pittman 1963: 186). Writing likewise derives from speech.

Oral composition can be a very valuable exercise....

Nevertheless, the skill with which this activity is handled depends largely on the control of the language suggested by the teacher and used by the children.... Only when the teacher is reasonably certain that learners can speak fairly correctly within the limits of their knowledge of sentence structure and vocabulary may he allow them free choice in sentence patterns and vocabulary. (Pittman 1963: 188)

The syllabus

Basic to the teaching of English in Situational Language Teaching is a structural syllabus and a word list. A structural syllabus is a list of the basic structures and sentence patterns of English, arranged according to their order of presentation. In Situational Language Teaching, structures are always taught within sentences, and vocabulary is chosen according to how well it enables sentence patterns to be taught. "Our early course will consist of a list of sentence patterns [statement patterns, question patterns, and request or command patterns]...will include as many structural words as possible, and sufficient content words to provide us with material upon which to base our language practice" (Frisby 1957: 134). Frisby gives an example of the typical structural syllabus around which situational teaching was based:

	Sentence pattern	*Vocabulary*
1st lesson	This is ...	book, pencil, ruler,
	That is ...	desk
2nd lesson	These are ...	chair, picture, door,
	Those are ...	window
3rd lesson	Is this ...? Yes it is.	watch, box, pen,
	Is that...? Yes it is.	blackboard

(1957:134)

The syllabus was not therefore a situational syllabus in the sense that this term is sometimes used (i.e., a list of situations and the language associated with them). Rather, situation refers to the manner of presenting and practicing sentence patterns, as we shall see later.

Types of learning and teaching activities

Situational Language Teaching employs a situational approach to presenting new sentence patterns and a drill-based manner of practicing them.

our method will...be situational. The situation will be controlled carefully to teach the new language material...in such a way that there can be no doubt in the learner's mind of the meaning of what he hears. ... almost all the vocabulary and structures taught in the first four or five years and even later can be placed in situations in which the meaning is quite clear. (Pittman 1963: 155–6)

By *situation* Pittman means the use of concrete objects, pictures, and realia, which together with actions and gestures can be used to demonstrate the meanings of new language items.

The form of new words and sentence patterns is demonstrated with examples and not through grammatical explanation or description. The meaning of new words and sentence patterns is not conveyed through translation. It is made clear visually (with objects, pictures, action and mime). Wherever possible model sentences are related and taken from a single situation. (Davies, Roberts, and Rossner 1975: 3)

The practice techniques employed generally consist of guided repetition and substitution activities, including chorus repetition, dictation, drills, and controlled oral-based reading and writing tasks. Other oral-practice techniques are sometimes used, including pair practice and group work.

Learner roles

In the initial stages of learning, the learner is required simply to listen and repeat what the teacher says and to respond to questions and commands. The learner has no control over the content of learning and is often regarded as likely to succumb to undesirable behaviors unless skillfully manipulated by the teacher. For example, the learner might lapse into faulty grammar or pronunciation, forget what has been taught, or fail to respond quickly enough; incorrect habits are to be avoided at all costs (see Pittman 1963). Later, more active participation is encouraged. This includes learners initiating responses and asking each other questions, although teacher-controlled introduction and practice of new language is stressed throughout (see Davies, Roberts, and Rossner 1975: 3–4).

Teacher roles

The teacher's function is threefold. In the presentation stage of the lesson, the teacher serves as a model, setting up situations in which the need for the target structure is created and then modeling the new structure for students to repeat. Then the teacher "becomes more like the skillful conductor of an orchestra, drawing the music out of the performers" (Byrne 1976: 2). The teacher is required to be a skillful manipulator, using questions, commands, and other cues to elicit correct sentences from the learners. Lessons are hence teacher directed, and the teacher sets the pace.

During the practice phase of the lesson, students are given more of an opportunity to use the language in less controlled situations, but the teacher is ever on the lookout for grammatical and structural errors that can form the basis of subsequent lessons. Organizing review is a primary task for the teacher according to Pittman (1963), who summarizes the teacher's responsibilities as dealing with

1. timing;
2. oral practice, to support the textbook structures;
3. revision [i.e., review];
4. adjustment to special needs of individuals;
5. testing;
6. developing language activities other than those arising from the textbook.
    (Pittman 1963: 177–8)

The teacher is essential to the success of the method, since the textbook is able only to describe activities for the teacher to carry out in class.

The role of instructional materials

Situational Language Teaching is dependent upon both a textbook and visual aids. The textbook contains tightly organized lessons planned around different grammatical structures. Visual aids may be produced by the teacher or may be commercially produced; they consist of wall charts, flashcards, pictures, stick figures, and so on. The visual element together with a carefully graded grammatical syllabus is a crucial aspect of Situational Language Teaching, hence the importance of the textbook. In principle, however, the textbook should be used "only as a guide to the learning process. The teacher is expected to be the master of his textbook" (Pittman 1963: 176).

Procedure

Classroom procedures in *Situational Language Teaching* vary according to the level of the class, but procedures at any level aim to move from controlled to freer practice of structures and from oral use of sentence patterns to their automatic use in speech, reading, and writing. Pittman gives an example of a typical lesson plan:

The first part of the lesson will be stress and intonation practice. . . . The main body of the lesson should then follow. This might consist of the teaching of a structure. If so, the lesson would then consist of four parts:

1. pronunciation
2. revision (to prepare for new work if necessary)
3. presentation of new structure or vocabulary

4. oral practice (drilling)
5. reading of material on the new structure, or written exercises.

(1963: 173)

Davies et al. give sample lesson plans for use with Situational Language Teaching. The structures being taught in the following lesson are "This is a ..." and "That's a..."

Teacher.   (holding up a watch) Look. This is a watch. (2×) (pointing to a clock on wall or table) That's a clock. (2×) That's a clock. (2×) This is a watch. (putting down watch and moving across to touch the clock or pick it up) This is a clock. (2×) (pointing to watch) That's a watch. (2×) (picking up a pen) This is a pen. (2×) (drawing large pencil on blackboard and moving away) That's a pencil. (2×) Take your pens. All take your pens. (students all pick up their pens)
Teacher.   Listen. This is a pen. (3×) This. (3×)
Students.   This. (3×)
A student. This. (6×)
Teacher.   This is a pen.
Students.   This is a pen. (3×)
Student.   (moving pen) This is a pen. (6×)
Teacher.   (pointing to blackboard) That's a pencil. (3×) That. (3×)
Students.   That. (3×)
A student. That. (6×)
Teacher.   That's a pencil.
Students.   (all pointing at blackboard) That's a pencil. (3×)
Student.   (pointing at blackboard) That's a pencil. (6×)
Teacher.   Take your books. (taking a book himself) This is a book. (3×)
Students.   This is a book. (3×)
Teacher.   (placing notebook in a visible place) Tell me...
Student 1. That's a notebook.

You can now begin taking objects out of your box, making sure they are as far as possible not new vocabulary items. Large objects may be placed in visible places at the front of the classroom. Smaller ones distributed to students."

(1975: 56)

These procedures illustrate the techniques used in presenting new language items in situations. Drills are likewise related to "situations." Pittman illustrates oral drilling on a pattern, using a box full of objects to create the situation. The pattern being practiced is "There's a NOUN + of + (noun) in the box." The teacher takes objects out of the box and the class repeats:

There's a tin of cigarettes in the box.
There's a packet of matches in the box.
There's a reel of cotton in the box.

There's a bottle of ink in the box.
There's a packet of pins in the box.
There's a pair of shoes in the box.
There's a jar of rice in the box.

(Pittman 1963: 168)

The teacher's kit, a collection of items and realia that can be used in situational language practice, is hence an essential part of the teacher's equipment.

Davies et al. likewise give detailed information about teaching procedures to be used with Situational Language Teaching. The sequence of activities they propose consists of:

1. Listening practice in which the teacher obtains his student's attention and repeats an example of the patterns or a word in isolation clearly, several times, probably saying it slowly at least once (where ... is ... the ... pen?), separating the words.
2. Choral imitation in which students all together or in large groups repeat what the teacher has said. This works best if the teacher gives a clear instruction like "Repeat," or "Everybody" and hand signals to mark time and stress.
3. Individual imitation in which the teacher asks several individual students to repeat the model he has given in order to check their pronunciation.
4. Isolation, in which the teacher isolates sounds, words or groups of words which cause trouble and goes through techniques 1–3 with them before replacing them in context.
5. Building up to a new model, in which the teacher gets students to ask and answer questions using patterns they already know in order to bring about the information necessary to introduce the new model.
6. Elicitation, in which the teacher, using mime, prompt words, gestures, etc., gets students to ask questions, make statements, or give new examples of the pattern.
7. Substitution drilling, in which the teacher uses cue words (words, pictures, numbers, names, etc.) to get individual students to mix the examples of the new patterns.
8. Question-answer drilling, in which the teacher gets one student to ask a question and another to answer until most students in the class have practiced asking and answering the new question form.
9. Correction, in which the teacher indicates by shaking his head, repeating the error, etc., that there is a mistake and invites the student or a different student to correct it. Where possible the teacher does not simply correct the mistake himself. He gets students to correct themselves so they will be encouraged to listen to each other carefully.

(Davies et al. 1975: 6–7)

Davies et al. then go on to discuss how follow-up reading and writing activities are to be carried out.

Conclusion

Procedures associated with Situational Language Teaching in the fifties and sixties are an extension and further development of well-established techniques advocated by proponents of the earlier Oral Approach in the British school of language teaching. They continue to be part of the standard set of procedures advocated in many current British methodology texts (e.g., Hubbard et al. 1983), and as we noted above, textbooks written according to the principles of Situational Language Teaching continue to be widely used in many parts of the world. In the mid-sixties, however, the view of language, language learning, and language teaching underlying Situational Language Teaching was called into question. We discuss this reaction and how it led to Communicative Language Teaching in Chapter 5. But because the principles of Situational Language Teaching, with its strong emphasis on oral practice, grammar, and sentence patterns, conform to the intuitions of many practically oriented classroom teachers, it continues to be widely used in the 1980s.

Bibliography

Alexander, L. G. 1967. *New Concept English*. 4 books. London: Longman.

Billows, F. L. 1961. *The Techniques of Language Teaching*. London: Longman.

Byrne, D. 1976. *Teaching Oral English*. London: Longman.

Coles, M., and B. Lord. 1975. *Access to English*. Oxford: Oxford University Press.

Commonwealth Office of Education. 1965. *Situational English*. London: Longman.

Davies, P., J. Roberts, and R. Rossner. 1975. *Situational Lesson Plans*. Mexico City: Macmillan.

Faucett, L., M. West, H. E. Palmer, and E. L. Thorndike. 1936. *The Interim Report on Vocabulary Selection for the Teaching of English as a Foreign Language*. London: P. S. King.

French, F. G. 1948–1950. *The Teaching of English Abroad*. 3 vols. Oxford: Oxford University Press.

Frisby, A. W. 1957. *Teaching English: Notes and Comments on Teaching English Overseas*. London: Longman.

Gatenby, E. V. 1944. *English as a Foreign Language*. London: Longman.

Gauntlett, J. O. 1957. *Teaching English as a Foreign Language*. London: Macmillan.

Gurrey, P. 1955. *Teaching English as a Foreign Language*. London: Longman.

Halliday, M. A. K., A. McIntosh, and P. Strevens. 1964. *The Linguistic Sciences and Language Teaching*. London: Longman.

Hartley, B., and P. Viney. 1979. *Streamline English*. Oxford: Oxford University Press.

Hodgson, F. M. 1955. *Learning Modern Languages*. London: Routledge and Kegan Paul.

Hornby, A. S. 1950. The situational approach in language teaching. A series of three articles in *English Language Teaching*. 4: 98–104, 121–8, 150–6.

Hornby, A. S. 1954. *A Guide to Patterns and Usage in English*. London: Oxford University Press.

Hornby, A. S. 1954–6. *Oxford Progressive English Course for Adult Learners*. 3 books. London: Oxford University Press.

Hornby, A. S., E. V. Gatenby, and H. Wakefield. 1953. *The Advanced Learner's Dictionary of Current English*. London: Oxford University Press.

Hubbard, P., H. Jones, B. Thornton, and R. Wheeler. 1983. *A Training Course for TEFL*. Oxford: Oxford University Press.

Jespersen, O. E. 1933. *Essentials of English Grammar*. London: Allen and Unwin.

Mennon, T. K. N., and M. S. Patel. 1957. *The Teaching of English as a Foreign Language*. Baroda, India: Acharya.

Morris, I. 1954. *The Art of Teaching English as a Living Language*. London: Macmillan.

O'Neill, R. 1973. *Kernel Lessons Plus*. London: Longman.

Palmer, H. E. 1917. *The Scientific Study and Teaching of Languages*. Reprinted. London: Oxford University Press, 1968.

Palmer, H. E. 1921. *Principles of Language Study*. New York: World Book Co.

Palmer, H. E. 1923. *The Oral Method of Teaching Languages*. Cambridge: Heffer.

Palmer, H. E. 1934. *Specimens of English Construction Patterns*. Tokyo: Department of Education.

Palmer, H. E. 1938. *Grammar of English Words*. London: Longman.

Palmer, H. E. 1940. *The Teaching of Oral English*. London: Longman.

Palmer, H. E., and F. G. Blandford. 1939. *A Grammar of Spoken English on a Strictly Phonetic Basis*. Cambridge: Heffer.

Pattison, B. 1952. *English Teaching in the World Today*. London: Evans.

Pattison, B. 1964. Modern methods of language teaching. *English Language Teaching* 19 (1): 2–6.

Pittman, G. 1963. *Teaching Structural English*. Brisbane: Jacaranda.

West, M. (ed.). 1953a. *A General Service List of English Words*. London: Longman.

West, M. 1953b. *The Teaching of English: A Guide to the New Method Series*. London: Longman.

Zandvoort, R. W. 1945. *A Handbook of English Grammar*. Groningen: Wolters.

4 The Audiolingual Method

Background

The Coleman Report in 1929 recommended a reading-based approach to foreign language teaching for use in American schools and colleges (Chapter 1). This emphasized teaching the comprehension of texts. Teachers taught from books containing short reading passages in the foreign language, preceded by lists of vocabulary. Rapid silent reading was the goal, but in practice teachers often resorted to discussing the content of the passage in English. Those involved in the teaching of English as a second language in the United States between the two world wars used either a modified Direct Method approach, a reading-based approach, or a reading-oral approach (Darian 1972). Unlike the approach that was being developed by British applied linguists during the same period, there was little attempt to treat language content systematically. Sentence patterns and grammar were introduced at the whim of the textbook writer. There was no standardization of the vocabulary or grammar that was included. Neither was there a consensus on what grammar, sentence patterns, and vocabulary were most important for beginning, intermediate, or advanced learners.

But the entry of the United States into World War II had a significant effect on language teaching in America. To supply the U.S. government with personnel who were fluent in German, French, Italian, Chinese, Japanese, Malay, and other languages, and who could work as interpreters, code-room assistants, and translators, it was necessary to set up a special language training program. The government commissioned American universities to develop foreign language programs for military personnel. Thus the Army Specialized Training Program (ASTP) was established in 1942. Fifty-five American universities were involved in the program by the beginning of 1943.

The objective of the army programs was for students to attain conversational proficiency in a variety of foreign languages. Since this was not the goal of conventional foreign language courses in the United States, new approaches were necessary. Linguists, such as Leonard Bloomfield at Yale, had already developed training programs as part of their linguistic research that were designed to give linguists and anthropologists mastery of American Indian languages and other languages they were studying. Textbooks did not exist for such languages. The technique Bloomfield and his colleagues used was sometimes known as the "informant method," since it used a native speaker of the language – the informant – who served as a source of phrases and vocabulary and who provided sentences for imitation, and a linguist, who supervised the learning experience. The linguist did not necessarily know the language but was trained in eliciting the basic structure of the language from the informant. Thus the students and the linguist were able to take part in guided conversation with the informant, and together they gradually learned how to speak the language, as well as to understand much of its basic grammar. Students in such courses studied ten hours a day, six days a week. There were generally fifteen hours of drill with native speakers and twenty to thirty hours of private study spread over two to three six-week sessions. This was the system adopted by the army, and in small classes of mature and highly motivated students, excellent results were often achieved.

The Army Specialized Training Program lasted only about two years but attracted considerable attention in the popular press and in the academic community. For the next ten years the "Army Method" and its suitability for use in regular language programs was discussed. But the linguists who developed the ASTP were not interested primarily in language teaching. The "methodology" of the Army Method, like the Direct Method, derived from the intensity of contact with the target language rather than from any well-developed methodological basis. It was a program innovative mainly in terms of the procedures used and the intensity of teaching rather than in terms of its underlying theory. However, it did convince a number of prominent linguists of the value of an intensive, oral-based approach to the learning of a foreign language.

Linguists and applied linguists during this period were becoming increasingly involved in the teaching of English as a foreign language. America had now emerged as a major international power. There was a growing demand for foreign expertise in the teaching of English. Thousands of foreign students entered the United States to study in universities, and many of these students required training in English before they could begin their studies. These factors led to the emergence of the American approach to ESL, which by the mid-fifties had become Audiolingualism.

In 1939 the University of Michigan developed the first English Language Institute in the United States; it specialized in the training of teachers of English as a foreign language and in teaching English as a second or foreign language. Charles Fries, director of the institute, was trained in structural linguistics, and he applied the principles of structural linguistics to language teaching. Fries and his colleagues rejected approaches like those of the Direct Method, in which learners are exposed to the language, use it, and gradually absorb its grammatical patterns. For Fries, grammar, or "structure," was the starting point. The structure of the language was identified with its basic sentence patterns and grammatical structures. The language was taught by systematic attention to pronunciation and by intensive oral drilling of its basic sentence patterns. Pattern practice was a basic classroom technique. "It is these basic patterns that constitute the learner's task. They require drill, drill, and more drill, and only enough vocabulary to make such drills possible" (Hockett 1959).

Michigan was not the only university involved in developing courses and materials for teaching English. A number of other similar programs were established, some of the earliest being at Georgetown University and American University, Washington, D.C., and at the University of Texas, Austin. U.S. linguists were becoming increasingly active, both within the United States and abroad, in supervising programs for the teaching of English (Moulton 1961). In 1950 the American Council of Learned Societies, under contract to the U.S. State Department, was commissioned to develop textbooks for teaching English to speakers of a wide number of foreign languages. The format the linguists involved in this project followed was known as the "general form": A lesson began with work on pronunciation, morphology, and grammar, followed by drills and exercises. The guidelines were published as *Structural Notes and Corpus: A Basis for the Preparation of Materials to Teach English as a Foreign Language* (American Council of Learned Societies 1952). This became an influential document and together with the "general form" was used as a guide to developing English courses for speakers of ten different languages (the famous *Spoken Language* series), published between 1953 and 1956 (Moulton 1961).

In many ways the methodology used by U.S. linguists and language teaching experts at this period sounded similar to the British Oral Approach, although the two traditions developed independently. The American approach differed, however, in its strong alliance with American structural linguistics and its applied linguistic applications, particularly contrastive analysis. Fries set forth his principles in *Teaching and Learning English as a Foreign Language* (1945), in which the problems of learning a foreign language were attributed to the conflict of different structural systems (i.e., differences between the grammatical and phonological patterns of the native tongue and the target language). Contrastive analysis of the two languages would allow potential problems of interference to be predicted and addressed through carefully prepared teaching materials. Thus was born a major industry in American applied linguistics − systematic comparisons of English with other languages, with a view toward solving the fundamental problems of foreign language learning.

The approach developed by linguists at Michigan and other universities became known variously as the Oral Approach, the Aural-Oral Approach, and the Structural Approach. It advocated aural training first, then pronunciation training, followed by speaking, reading, and writing. Language was identified with speech, and speech was approached through structure. This approach influenced the way languages were taught in the United States throughout the fifties. As an approach to the teaching of English as a foreign language the new orthodoxy was promoted through the University of Michigan's journal *Language Learning*. This was a period when expertise in linguistics was regarded as a necessary and sufficient foundation for expertise in language teaching. Not surprisingly, the classroom materials produced by Fries and linguists at Yale, Cornell, and elsewhere evidenced considerable linguistic analysis but very little pedagogy. They were widely used, however, and the applied linguistic principles on which they were based were thought to incorporate the most advanced scientific approach to language teaching. If there was any learning theory underlying the Aural-Oral materials, it was a commonsense application of the idea that practice makes perfect. There is no explicit reference to then-current learning theory in Fries's work. It was the incorporation of the linguistic principles of the Aural-Oral approach with state-of-the-art psychological learning theory in the mid-fifties that led to the method that came to be known as Audiolingualism.

The emergence of the Audiolingual Method resulted from the increased attention given to foreign language teaching in the United States toward the end of the 1950s. The need for a radical change and rethinking of foreign language teaching methodology (most of which was still linked to the Reading Method) was prompted by the launching of the first Russian satellite in 1957. The U.S. Government acknowledged the need for a more intensive effort to teach foreign languages in order to prevent Americans from becoming isolated from scientific advances made in other countries. The National Defense Education Act (1958), among other measures, provided funds for the study and analysis of modern languages, for the development of teaching materials, and for the training of teachers. Teachers were encouraged to attend summer institutes to improve their knowledge of foreign languages and to learn the principles of linguistics and the new linguistically based teaching methods. Language teaching specialists set about developing a method that was applicable to conditions in U.S. colleges and university classrooms. They drew on the earlier experience of the army programs and the Aural-Oral or Structural Approach developed by Fries and his colleagues, adding insights taken from behaviorist psychology. This combination of structural linguistic theory, contrastive analysis, aural-oral procedures, and behaviorist psychology led to the Audiolingual Method. Audiolingualism (the term was coined by Professor Nelson Brooks in 1964) claimed to have transformed language teaching from an art to a science, which would enable learners to achieve mastery of a foreign language effectively and efficiently. The method was widely adopted for teaching foreign languages in North American colleges and universities. It provided the methodological foundation for materials for the teaching of foreign languages at college and university level in the United States and Canada, and its principles formed the basis of such widely used series as the *Lado English Series* (Lado 1977) and *English 900* (English Language Services 1964). Although the method began to fall from favor in the late sixties for reasons we shall discuss later, Audiolingualism and materials based on audiolingual principles continue to be widely used today. Let us examine the features of the Audiolingual Method at the levels of approach, design, and procedure.

Approach

Theory of language

The theory of language underlying Audiolingualism was derived from a view proposed by American linguists in the 1950s – a view that came to be known as *structural linguistics*. Linguistics had emerged as a flourishing academic discipline in the 1950s, and the structural theory of language constituted its backbone. Structural linguistics had developed in part as a reaction to traditional grammar. Traditional approaches to the study of language had linked the study of language to philosophy and to a mentalist approach to grammar. Grammar was considered a branch of logic, and the grammatical categories of Indo-European languages were thought to represent ideal categories in languages. Many nineteenth-century language scholars had viewed modern European languages as corruptions of classical grammar, and languages from other parts of the world were viewed as primitive and underdeveloped.

The reaction against traditional grammar was prompted by the movement toward positivism and empiricism, which Darwin's *Origin of the Species* had helped promote, and by an increased interest in non-European languages on the part of scholars. A more practical interest in language study emerged. As linguists discovered new sound types and new patterns of linguistic invention and organization, a new interest in phonetics, phonology, morphology, and syntax developed. By the 1930s, the scientific approach to the study of language was thought to consist of collecting examples of what speakers said and analyzing them according to different levels of structural organization rather than according to categories of Latin grammar. A sophisticated methodology for collecting and analyzing data developed, which involved transcribing spoken utterances in a language phonetically and later working out the phonemic, morphological (stems, prefixes, suffixes, etc.), and syntactic (phrases, clauses, sentence types) systems underlying the grammar of the language. Language was viewed as a system of structurally related elements for the encoding of meaning, the elements being phonemes, morphemes, words, structures, and sentence types. The term *structural* referred to these characteristics: (a) Elements in a language were thought of as being linearly produced in a rule-governed (structured) way. (b) Language samples could be exhaustively described at any structural level of description (phonetic, phonemic, morphological, etc.). (c) Linguistic levels were thought of as systems within systems – that is, as being pyramidally structured; phonemic systems led to morphemic systems, and these in turn led to the higher-level systems of phrases, clauses, and sentences.

Learning a language, it was assumed, entails mastering the elements or building blocks of the language and learning the rules by which these elements are combined, from phoneme to morpheme to word to phrase to sentence. The phonological system defines those sound elements that contrast meaningfully with one another in the language (phonemes), their phonetic realizations in specific environments (allophones), and their permissible sequences (phonotactics). The phonological and grammatical systems of the language constitute the organization of language and by implication the units of production and comprehension. The grammatical system consists of a listing of grammatical elements and rules for their linear combination into words, phrases, and sentences. Rule-ordered processes involve addition, deletion, and transposition of elements.

An important tenet of structural linguistics was that the primary medium of language is oral: Speech is language. Since many languages do not have a written form and we learn to speak before we learn to read or write, it was argued that language is "primarily what is spoken and only secondarily what is written" (Brooks 1964). Therefore, it was assumed that speech had a priority in language teaching. This was contrary to popular views of the relationship of the spoken and written forms of language, since it had been widely assumed that language existed principally as symbols written on paper, and that spoken language was an imperfect realization of the pure written version.

This scientific approach to language analysis appeared to offer the foundations for a scientific approach to language teaching. In 1961 the American linguist William Moulton, in a report prepared for the 9th International Congress of Linguists, proclaimed the linguistic principles on which language teaching methodology should be based: "Language is speech, not writing.... A language is a set of habits.... Teach the language, not about the language.... A language is what its native speak-

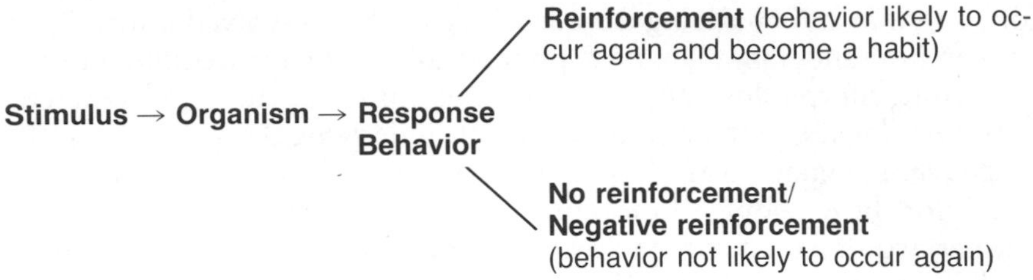

Reinforcement (behavior likely to occur again and become a habit)

Stimulus → Organism → Response
Behavior

No reinforcement/
Negative reinforcement
(behavior not likely to occur again)

Figure 4.1

ers say, not what someone thinks they ought to say.... Languages are different" (quoted in Rivers 1964: 5). But a method cannot be based simply on a theory of language. It also needs to refer to the psychology of learning and to learning theory. It is to this aspect of Audiolingualism that we now turn.

Theory of learning

The language teaching theoreticians and methodologists who developed Audiolingualism not only had a convincing and powerful theory of language to draw upon but they were also working in a period when a prominent school of American psychology – known as behavioral psychology – claimed to have tapped the secrets of all human learning, including language learning. Behaviorism, like structural linguistics, is another antimentalist, empirically based approach to the study of human behavior. To the behaviorist, the human being is an organism capable of a wide repertoire of behaviors. The occurrence of these behaviors is dependent upon three crucial elements in learning: a *stimulus*, which serves to elicit behavior; a *response* triggered by a stimulus; and *reinforcement*, which serves to mark the response as being appropriate (or inappropriate) and encourages the repetition (or suppression) of the response in the future (see Skinner 1957; Brown 1980). A representation of this can be seen in Figure 4.1.

Reinforcement is a vital element in the learning process, because it increases the likelihood that the behavior will occur again and eventually become a habit. To apply this theory to language learning is to identify the organism as the foreign language learner, the behavior as verbal behavior, the stimulus as what is taught or presented of the foreign language, the response as the learner's reaction to the stimulus, and the reinforcement as the extrinsic approval and praise of the teacher or fellow students or the intrinsic self-satisfaction of target language use. Language mastery is represented as acquiring a set of appropriate language stimulus-response chains.

The descriptive practices of structural linguists suggested a number of hypotheses about language learning, and hence about language teaching as well. For example, since linguists normally described languages beginning with the phonological level and finishing with the sentence level, it was assumed that this was also the appropriate sequence for learning and teaching. Since speech was now held to be primary and writing secondary, it was assumed that language teaching should focus on mastery of speech and that writing or even written prompts should be withheld until reasonably late in the language learning process. Since the structure is what is important and unique about a language, early practice should focus on mastery of phonological and grammatical structures rather than on mastery of vocabulary.

Out of these various influences emerged a number of learning principles, which became the psychological foundations of Audiolingualism and came to shape its methodological practices. Among the more central are the following:

1. Foreign language learning is basically a process of mechanical habit formation. Good habits are formed by giving correct responses rather than by making mistakes. By memorizing dialogues and performing pattern drills the chances of producing mistakes are minimized. Language is verbal behavior – that is, the automatic production and comprehension of utterances – and can be learned by inducing the students to do likewise.
2. Language skills are learned more effectively if the items to be learned in the target language are presented in spoken form before they are seen in written form. Aural-oral training is needed to provide the foundation for the development of other language skills.
3. Analogy provides a better foundation for language learning than analysis. Analogy involves the processes of generalization and discrimination. Explanations of rules are therefore not given until students have practiced a pattern in a variety of contexts and are thought to have acquired a perception of the analogies involved. Drills can enable learners to form correct analogies. Hence the approach to the teaching of grammar is essentially inductive rather than deductive.
4. The meanings that the words of a language have for the native speaker can be learned only in a linguistic and cultural context and not in isolation. Teaching a language thus involves teaching aspects of the cultural system of the people who speak the language (Rivers 1964: 19–22).

In advocating these principles, proponents of Audiolingualism were drawing on the theory of a well-developed school of American psychology – behaviorism. The prominent Harvard behaviorist B. F. Skinner had elaborated a theory of learning applicable to language learning in his influential book *Verbal Behavior* (1957), in which he stated, "We have no reason to assume... that verbal behavior differs in any fundamental respect from non-verbal behavior, or that any new principles must be invoked to account for it" (1957: 10). Armed with a powerful theory of the nature of language and of language learning, audiolingualists could now turn to the design of language teaching courses and materials.

Design

Audiolingualists demanded a complete reorientation of the foreign language curriculum. Like the nineteenth-century reformers, they advocated a return to speech-based instruction with the primary objective of oral proficiency, and dismissed the study of grammar or literature as the goal of foreign language teaching. "A radical transformation is called for, a new orientation of procedures is demanded, and a thorough house cleaning of methods, materials, texts and tests is unavoidable" (Brooks 1964: 50).

Objectives

Brooks distinguishes between short-range and long-range objectives of an audiolingual program. Short-range objectives include training in listening comprehension, accurate pronunciation, recognition of speech symbols as graphic signs on the printed page, and ability to reproduce these symbols in writing (Brooks 1964: 111). "These immediate objectives imply three others: first, control of the structures of sound, form, and order in the new language; second, acquaintance with vocabulary items that bring content into these structures; and third, meaning, in terms of the significance these verbal symbols have for those who speak the language natively" (Brooks 1964: 113). Long-range objectives "must be language as the native speaker uses it. . . . There must be some knowledge of a second language as it is possessed by a true bilingualist" (Brooks 1964: 107).

In practice this means that the focus in the early stages is on oral skills, with gradual links to other skills as learning develops. Oral proficiency is equated with accurate pronunciation and grammar and the ability to respond quickly and accurately in speech situations. The teaching of listening comprehension, pronunciation, grammar, and vocabulary are all related to development of oral fluency. Reading and writing skills may be taught, but they are dependent upon prior oral skills. Language is primarily speech in audiolingual theory, but speaking skills are themselves dependent upon the ability to accurately perceive and produce the major phonological features of the target language, fluency in the use of the key grammatical patterns in the language, and knowledge of sufficient vocabulary to use with these patterns.

The syllabus

Audiolingualism is a linguistic, or structure-based, approach to language teaching. The starting point is a linguistic syllabus, which contains the key items of phonology, morphology, and syntax of the language arranged according to their order of presentation. These may have been derived in part from a *contrastive analysis* of the differences between the native tongue and the target language, since these differences are thought to be the cause of the major difficulties the learner will encounter. In addition, a lexical syllabus of basic vocabulary items is also usually specified in advance. In *Foundations for English Teaching* (Fries and Fries 1961), for example, a corpus of structural and lexical items graded into three levels is proposed, together with suggestions as to the situations that could be used to contextualize them.

The language skills are taught in the order of listening, speaking, reading, and writing. Listening is viewed largely as training in aural discrimination of basic sound patterns. The language may be presented entirely orally at first; written representations are usually withheld from learners in early stages.

The learner's activities must at first be confined to the audiolingual and gestural-visual bands of language behavior....
Recognition and discrimination are followed by imitation, repetition and memorization. Only when he is thoroughly familiar with sounds, arrangements, and forms does he center his attention on enlarging his vocabulary....
Throughout he concentrates upon gaining accuracy before striving for fluency. (Brooks 1964: 50)

When reading and writing are introduced, students are taught to read and write what they have already learned to say orally. An attempt is made to minimize the possibilities for making mistakes both in speaking and writing by using a tightly structured approach to the presentation of new language items. At more advanced levels, more complex reading and writing tasks may be introduced.

Types of learning and teaching activities

Dialogues and drills form the basis of audiolingual classroom practices. Dialogues provide the means of contextualizing key structures and illustrate situations in which structures might be used as well as some cultural aspects of the target language. Dialogues are used for repetition and memorization. Correct pronunciation, stress, rhythm, and intonation are emphasized. After a dialogue has been presented and memorized, specific grammatical patterns in the dialogue are selected and become the focus of various kinds of drill and pattern-practice exercises.

The use of drills and pattern practice is a distinctive feature of the Audiolingual Method. Various kinds of drills are used. Brooks (1964: 156–61) includes the following:

1. *Repetition*. The student repeats an utterance aloud as soon as he has heard it. He does this without looking at a printed text. The utterance must be brief enough to be retained by the ear. Sound is as important as form and order.

   EXAMPLE.
   This is the seventh month. –This is the seventh month.
   After a student has repeated an utterance, he may repeat it again and add a few words, then repeat that whole utterance and add more words.

   EXAMPLES.
   I used to know him. –I used to know him.
   I used to know him *years ago*. –I used to know him *years ago when we were in school*. . . .

2. *Inflection*. One word in an utterance appears in another form when repeated.

   EXAMPLES.
   I bought the *ticket*. –I bought the *tickets*.
   He bought the candy. –*She* bought the candy.
   I called the young *man*. –I called the young *men*. . . .

3. *Replacement*. One word in an utterance is replaced by another.

   EXAMPLES.
   He bought this *house* cheap. –He bought *it* cheap.
   Helen left early –*She* left early.
   They gave their *boss* a watch. –They gave *him* a watch. . . .

4. *Restatement*. The student rephrases an utterance and addresses it to someone else, according to instructions.

   EXAMPLES.
   Tell him to wait for you. –Wait for me.
   Ask her how old she is. –How old are you?
   Ask John when he began. –John, when did you begin? . . .

5. *Completion*. The student hears an utterance that is complete except for one word, then repeats the utterance in completed form.

   EXAMPLES.
   I'll go my way and you go. . . . –I'll go my way and you go *yours*.
   We all have . . . own troubles. –We all have *our* own troubles. . . .

6. *Transposition*. A change in word order is necessary when a word is added.

   EXAMPLES.
   I'm hungry. (so). –So *am* I.
   I'll never do it again. (neither). –Neither *will* I. . . .

7. *Expansion.* When a word is added it takes a certain place in the sequence.

   EXAMPLES.
   I know him. (hardly). –I *hardly* know him.
   I know him. (well). –I know him *well*. . . .

8. *Contraction.* A single word stands for a phrase or clause.

   EXAMPLES.
   Put your hand *on the table*. –Put your hand *there*.
   They believe *that the earth is flat*. –They believe *it*. . . .

9. *Transformation.* A sentence is transformed by being made negative or interrogative or through changes in tense, mood, voice, aspect, or modality.

   EXAMPLES.
   He knows my address.
   He doesn't know my address.
   Does he know my address?
   He used to know my address.
   If he had known my address.

10. *Integration.* Two separate utterances are integrated into one.

    EXAMPLES.
    They must be honest. This is important. –It is important that they be honest.
    I know that man. He is looking for you. –I know the man who is looking for you. . . .

11. *Rejoinder.* The student makes an appropriate rejoinder to a given utterance. He is told in advance to respond in one of the following ways:

    Be polite.
    Answer the question.
    Agree.
    Agree emphatically.
    Express surprise.
    Express regret.
    Disagree.
    Disagree emphatically.
    Question what is said.
    Fail to understand.

    BE POLITE. EXAMPLES.
    Thank you. –You're welcome.
    May I take one? –Certainly.

    ANSWER THE QUESTION. EXAMPLES.
    What is your name? –My name is Smith.
    Where did it happen? –In the middle of the street.

AGREE.   EXAMPLES.
He's following us. —I think you're right.
This is good coffee. —It's very good.
. . . .

12. *Restoration.* The student is given a sequence of words that have been culled from a sentence but still bear its basic meaning. He uses these words with a minimum of changes and additions to restore the sentence to its original form. He may be told whether the time is present, past, or future.

EXAMPLES.
students/waiting/bus —The students are waiting for the bus.
boys/build/house/tree —The boys built a house in a tree. . . .

Learner roles

Learners are viewed as organisms that can be directed by skilled training techniques to produce correct responses. In accordance with behaviorist learning theory, teaching focuses on the external manifestations of learning rather than on the internal processes. Learners play a reactive role by responding to stimuli, and thus have little control over the content, pace, or style of learning. They are not encouraged to initiate interaction, because this may lead to mistakes. The fact that in the early stages learners do not always understand the meaning of what they are repeating is not perceived as a drawback, for by listening to the teacher, imitating accurately, and responding to and performing controlled tasks they are learning a new form of verbal behavior.

Teacher roles

In Audiolingualism, as in Situational Language Teaching, the teacher's role is central and active; it is a teacher-dominated method. The teacher models the target language, controls the direction and pace of learning, and monitors and corrects the learners' performance. The teacher must keep the learners attentive by varying drills and tasks and choosing relevant situations to practice structures. Language learning is seen to result from active verbal interaction between the teacher and the learners. Failure to learn results only from the improper application of the method, for example, from the teacher not providing sufficient practice or from the learner not memorizing the essential patterns and structures; but the method itself is never to blame. Brooks argues that the teacher must be trained to do the following:

Introduce, sustain, and harmonize the learning of the four skills in this order: hearing, speaking, reading and writing.
Use — and not use — English in the language classroom.

Model the various types of language behavior that the student is to learn.
Teach spoken language in dialogue form.
Direct choral response by all or parts of the class.
Teach the use of structure through pattern practice.
Guide the student in choosing and learning vocabulary.
Show how words relate to meaning in the target language.
Get the individual student to talk.
Reward trials by the student in such a way that learning is reinforced.
Teach a short story and other literary forms.
Establish and maintain a cultural island.
Formalize on the first day the rules according to which the language class is
    to be conducted, and enforce them.

(Brooks 1964: 143)

The role of instructional materials

Instructional materials in the Audiolingual Method assist the teacher to develop language mastery in the learner. They are primarily teacher oriented. A student textbook is often not used in the elementary phases of a course where students are primarily listening, repeating, and responding. At this stage in learning, exposure to the printed word may not be considered desirable, because it distracts attention from the aural input. The teacher, however, will have access to a teacher's book that contains the structured sequence of lessons to be followed and the dialogues, drills, and other practice activities. When textbooks and printed materials are introduced to the student, they provide the texts of dialogues and cues needed for drills and exercises.

Tape recorders and audiovisual equipment often have central roles in an audiolingual course. If the teacher is not a native speaker of the target language, the tape recorder provides accurate models for dialogues and drills. A language laboratory may also be considered essential. It provides the opportunity for further drill work and to receive controlled error-free practice of basic structures. It also adds variety by providing an alternative to classroom practice. A taped lesson may first present a dialogue for listening practice, allow for the student to repeat the sentences in the dialogue line by line, and provide follow-up fluency drills on grammar or pronunciation.

Procedure

Since Audiolingualism is primarily an oral approach to language teaching, it is not surprising that the process of teaching involves extensive oral instruction. The focus of instruction is on immediate and accurate speech; there is little provision for grammatical explanation or talking about the language. As far as possible, the target language is used as the medium of instruction, and translation or use of the native tongue is discouraged. Classes of ten or less are considered optimal, although larger classes are often the norm. Brooks lists the following procedures the teacher should adopt in using the Audiolingual Method:

The modeling of all learnings by the teacher.

The subordination of the mother tongue to the second language by rendering English inactive while the new language is being learned.

The early and continued training of the ear and tongue without recourse to graphic symbols.

The learning of structure through the practice of patterns of sound, order, and form, rather than by explanation.

The gradual substitution of graphic symbols for sounds after sounds are thoroughly known.

The summarizing of the main principles of structure for the student's use when the structures are already familiar, especially when they differ from those of the mother tongue....

The shortening of the time span between a performance and the pronouncement of its rightness or wrongness, without interrupting the response. This enhances the factor of reinforcement in learning.

The minimizing of vocabulary until all common structures have been learned.

The study of vocabulary only in context.

Sustained practice in the use of the language only in the molecular form of speaker-hearer-situation.

Practice in translation only as a literary exercise at an advanced level.

(Brooks 1964: 142)

In a typical audiolingual lesson the following procedures would be observed:

1. Students first hear a model dialogue (either read by the teacher or on tape) containing the key structures that are the focus of the lesson. They repeat each line of the dialogue, individually and in chorus. The teacher pays attention to pronunciation, intonation, and fluency. Correction of mistakes of pronunciation or grammar is direct and immediate. The dialogue is memorized gradually, line by line. A line may be broken down into several phrases if necessary. The dialogue is read aloud in chorus, one half saying one speaker's part and the other half responding. The students do not consult their book throughout this phase.
2. The dialogue is adapted to the students' interest or situation, through changing certain key words or phrases. This is acted out by the students.
3. Certain key structures from the dialogue are selected and used as the basis for pattern drills of different kinds. These are first practiced in chorus and then individually. Some grammatical explanation may be offered at this point, but this is kept to an absolute minimum.
4. The students may refer to their textbook, and follow-up reading, writing, or vocabulary activities based on the dialogue may be introduced. At the beginning level, writing is purely imitative and consists of little more than

copying out sentences that have been practiced. As proficiency increases, students may write out variations of structural items they have practiced or write short compositions on given topics with the help of framing questions, which will guide their use of the language.

5. Follow-up activities may take place in the language laboratory, where further dialogue and drill work is carried out.

The decline of Audiolingualism

Audiolingualism reached its period of most widespread use in the 1960s and was applied both to the teaching of foreign languages in the United States and to the teaching of English as a second or foreign language. It led to such widely used courses as *English 900* and the *Lado English Series*, as well as to texts for teaching the major European languages. But then came criticism on two fronts. On the one hand, the theoretical foundations of Audiolingualism were attacked as being unsound both in terms of language theory and learning theory. On the other, practitioners found that the practical results fell short of expectations. Students were often found to be unable to transfer skills acquired through Audiolingualism to real communication outside the classroom, and many found the experience of studying through audiolingual procedures to be boring and unsatisfying.

The theoretical attack on audiolingual beliefs resulted from changes in American linguistic theory in the sixties. The MIT linguist Noam Chomsky rejected the structuralist approach to language description as well as the behaviorist theory of language learning. "Language is not a habit structure. Ordinary linguistic behavior characteristically involves innovation, formation of new sentences and patterns in accordance with rules of great abstractness and intricacy" (Chomsky 1966: 153). Chomsky's theory of transformational grammar proposed that the fundamental properties of language derive from innate aspects of the mind and from how humans process experience through language. His theories were to revolutionize American linguistics and focus the attention of linguists and psychologists on the mental properties people bring to bear on language use and language learning. Chomsky also proposed an alternative theory of language learning to that of the behaviorists. Behaviorism regarded language learning as similar in principle to any other kind of learning. It was subject to the same laws of stimulus and response, reinforcement and association. Chomsky argued that such a learning theory could not possibly serve as a model of how humans learn language, since much of human language use is not imitated behavior but is created anew from underlying knowledge of abstract rules. Sentences are not learned by imitation and repetition but "generated" from the learner's underlying "competence."

Suddenly the whole audiolingual paradigm was called into question: pattern practice, drilling, memorization. These might lead to language-like behaviors, but they were not resulting in competence. This created a crisis in American language teaching circles from which a full recovery has not yet been made. Temporary relief was offered in the form of a theory derived in part from Chomsky – cognitive code learning. In 1966 John B. Carroll, a psychologist who had taken a close interest in foreign language teaching, wrote:

The audio-lingual habit theory which is so prevalent in American foreign language teaching was, perhaps fifteen years ago in step with the state of psychological thinking of that time, but it is no longer abreast of recent developments. It is ripe for major revision, particularly in the direction of joining it with some of the better elements of the cognitive-code learning theory. (Carroll 1966: 105)

This referred to a view of learning that allowed for a conscious focus on grammar and that acknowledged the role of abstract mental processes in learning rather than defining learning simply in terms of habit formation. Practice activities should involve meaningful learning and language use. Learners should be encouraged to use their innate and creative abilities to derive and make explicit the underlying grammatical rules of the language. For a time in the early seventies there was a considerable interest in the implication of the cognitive-code theory for language teaching (e.g., see Jakobovits 1970; Lugton 1971). But no clear-cut methodological guidelines emerged, nor did any particular method incorporating this view of learning. The term *cognitive code* is still sometimes invoked to refer to any conscious attempt to organize materials around a grammatical syllabus while allowing for meaningful practice and use of language. The lack of an alternative to Audiolingualism in language teaching in the United States has led to a period of adaptation, innovation, experimentation, and some confusion. On the one hand are new methods that have been developed independently of current linguistic and second language acquisition theory (e.g., Total Physical Response, Silent Way, Counseling-Learning); on the other are competing approaches that are derived, it is claimed, from contemporary theories of language and second language acquisition (e.g., The Natural Approach, Communicative Language Teaching). These developments will be considered in the remaining chapters of this book.

Conclusion

Audiolingualism holds that language learning is like other forms of learning. Since language is a formal, rule-governed system, it can be formally organized to maximize teaching and learning efficiency. Audiolingualism thus stresses the mechanistic aspects of language learning and language use.

There are many similarities between Situational Language Teaching and Audiolingualism. The order in which the language skills are introduced, and the focus on accuracy through drill and practice in the basic structures and sentence patterns of the target language, might suggest that these methods drew from each other. In fact, however, Situational Language Teaching was a development of the earlier Direct Method (see Chapter 1) and does not have the strong ties to linguistics and behavioral psychology that characterize Audiolingualism. The similarities of the two methods reflect similar views about the nature of language and of language learning, though these views were in fact developed from quite different traditions.

Bibliography

Allen, V. F. 1965. *On Teaching English to Speakers of Other Languages*. Champaign, Ill.: National Council of Teachers of English.

American Council of Learned Societies. 1952. *Structural Notes and Corpus: A Basis for the Preparation of Materials to Teach English as a Foreign Language*. Washington, D.C.: American Council of Learned Societies.

Bloch, B., and G. Trager. 1942. *Outline of Linguistic Analysis*. Baltimore: Linguistic Society of America.

Bloomfield, L. 1933. *Language*. New York: Holt.

Brooks, N. 1964. *Language and Language Learning: Theory and Practice*. 2nd ed. New York: Harcourt Brace.

Brown, H. D. 1980. *Principles of Language Learning and Teaching*. Englewood Cliffs, N.J.: Prentice-Hall.

Carroll, J. B. 1953. *The Study of Language: A Survey of Linguistics and Related Disciplines in America*. Cambridge, Mass.: Harvard University Press.

Carroll, J. B. 1966a. *Research in Foreign Language Teaching: The Last Five Years*. In R. G. Mead, Jr. (ed.), *Language Teaching: Broader Contexts*, pp. 12–42. Northeast Conference Reports on the Teaching of Foreign Languages: Reports of the Working Committees. New York: MLA Materials Center.

Carroll, J. B. 1966b. The contributions of psychological theory and educational research to the teaching of foreign languages. In A. Valdman (ed.), *Trends in Language Teaching*, pp. 93–106. New York: McGraw-Hill.

Chastain, K. 1969. The audio-lingual habit theory versus the cognitive code-learning theory: some theoretical considerations. *International Review of Applied Linguistics* 7: 79–106.

Chastain, K. 1971. *The Development of Modern Language Skills: Theory to Practice*. Chicago: Rand McNally.

Chomsky, N. 1957. *Syntactic Structures*. The Hague: Mouton.

Chomsky, N. 1959. A review of B. F. Skinner's *Verbal Behavior*. *Language* 35(1): 26–58.

Chomsky, N. 1965. *Aspects of the Theory of Syntax*. Cambridge, Mass.: MIT Press.

Chomsky, N. 1966. Linguistic theory. Reprinted in J. P. B. Allen and P. Van Buren (eds.), *Chomsky: Selected Readings*, pp. 152–9. London: Oxford University Press.

Darian, S. G. 1972. *English as a Foreign Language: History, Development, and Methods of Teaching*. Norman: University of Oklahoma Press.

English Language Services. 1964. *English 900*. New York: Collier Macmillan.

Fries, C. C. 1945. *Teaching and Learning English as a Foreign Language*. Ann Arbor: University of Michigan Press.

Fries, C. C., and A. C. Fries. 1961. *Foundations for English Teaching*. Tokyo: Kenkyusha.

Gagne, R. M. 1962. Military training and principles of learning. *American Psychologist* 17(2): 83–91.

Hilgard, E. R. 1975. *Theories of Learning*. 2nd ed. New York: Appleton-Century-Crofts.

Hockett, C. F. 1958. *A Course in Modern Linguistics*. New York: Macmillan.

Hockett, C. F. 1959. The objectives and process of language teaching. Reprinted in D. Byrne (ed.), *English Teaching Extracts*. London: Longman, 1969.

Hughes, J. P. 1968. *Linguistics and Language Teaching*. New York: Random House.

Jakobovits, L. A. 1970. *Foreign Language Learning: A Psycholinguistic Analysis of the Issues*. Rowley, Mass.: Newbury House.

Lado, R. 1957. *Linguistics Across Cultures: Applied Linguistics for Language Teachers*. Ann Arbor: University of Michigan Press.

Lado, R. 1961. *Language Testing*. London: Longman.

Lado, R. 1977. *Lado English Series*. 7 books. New York: Regents.

Lugton, R. (ed.). 1971. *Toward a Cognitive Approach to Second Language Acquisition*. Philadelphia: Center for Curriculum Development.

Matthew, R. J. 1947. *Language and Area Studies in the Armed Services: Their Future and Significance*. Washington: American Council on Education.

Modern Language Association. 1962. *Reports of Surveys and Studies in the Teaching of Modern Foreign Languages*. New York: Modern Language Teaching Association.

Moulton, W. G. 1961. Linguistics and language teaching in the United States: 1940–1960. In C. Mohrmann, A. Sommerfelt, and J. Whatmough (eds.), *Trends in European and American Linguistics, 1930–1960*, pp. 82–109. Utrecht: Spectrum.

Moulton, W. G. 1963. What is structural drill? *International Journal of American Linguistics* 29 (2, pt. 3): 3–15.

Moulton, W. 1966. *A Linguistic Guide to Language Learning*. New York: Modern Language Association.

Parker, W. 1962. *The National Interest and Foreign Languages*. Washington, D.C.: Department of State.

Rivers, W. M. 1964. *The Psychologist and the Foreign Language Teacher*. Chicago: University of Chicago Press.

Rivers, W. M. 1981. *Teaching Foreign Language Skills*. Chicago: University of Chicago Press.

Skinner, B. F. 1957. *Verbal Behavior*. New York: Appleton-Century-Crofts.

Smith, H. L. 1956. *Linguistic Science and the Teaching of English*. Cambridge, Mass.: Harvard University Press.

Stack, E. 1969. *The Language Laboratory and Modern Language Teaching*. New York: Oxford University Press.

Stern, H. H. 1983. *Fundamental Concepts of Language Teaching*. Oxford: Oxford University Press.

United States Office of Education. 1963. *The Language Development Program*. Washington, D.C.: U.S. Government Printing Office.

5 Communicative Language Teaching

Background

The origins of Communicative Language Teaching (CLT) are to be found in the changes in the British language teaching tradition dating from the late 1960s. Until then, Situational Language Teaching (see Chapter 3) represented the major British approach to teaching English as a foreign language. In Situational Language Teaching, language was taught by practicing basic structures in meaningful situation-based activities. But just as the linguistic theory underlying Audiolingualism was rejected in the United States in the mid-1960s, British applied linguists began to call into question the theoretical assumptions underlying Situational Language Teaching:

> By the end of the sixties it was clear that the situational approach . . . had run its course. There was no future in continuing to pursue the chimera of predicting language on the basis of situational events. What was required was a closer study of the language itself and a return to the traditional concept that utterances carried meaning in themselves and expressed the meanings and intentions of the speakers and writers who created them. (Howatt 1984: 280)

This was partly a response to the sorts of criticisms the prominent American linguist Noam Chomsky had leveled at structural linguistic theory in his now classic book *Syntactic Structures* (1957). Chomsky had demonstrated that the current standard structural theories of language were incapable of accounting for the fundamental characteristic of language – the creativity and uniqueness of individual sentences. British applied linguists emphasized another fundamental dimension of language that was inadequately addressed in current approaches to language teaching at that time – the functional and communicative potential of language. They saw the need to focus in language teaching on communicative proficiency rather than on mere mastery of structures. Scholars who advocated this view of language, such as Christopher Candlin and Henry Widdowson, drew on the work of British functional linguists (e.g., John Firth, M. A. K. Halliday), American work in sociolinguistics (e.g. Dell Hymes, John Gumperz, and William Labov), as well as work in philosophy (e.g., John Austin and John Searle).

Another impetus for different approaches to foreign language teaching came from changing educational realities in Europe. With the increasing interdependence of European countries came the need for greater efforts to teach adults the major languages of the European Common Market and the Council of Europe, a regional organization for cultural and educational cooperation. Education was one of the Council of Europe's major areas of activity. It sponsored international conferences on language teaching, published monographs and books about language teaching, and was active in promoting the formation of the International Association of Applied Linguistics. The need to articulate and develop alternative methods of language teaching was considered a high priority.

In 1971 a group of experts began to investigate the possibility of developing language courses on a unit-credit system, a system in which learning tasks are broken down into "portions or units, each of which corresponds to a component of a learner's needs and is systematically related to all the other portions" (van Ek and Alexander 1980: 6). The group used studies of the needs of European language learners, and in particular a preliminary document prepared by a British linguist, D. A. Wilkins (1972), which proposed a functional or communicative definition of language that could serve as a basis for developing communicative syllabuses for language teaching. Wilkins's contribution was an analysis of the communicative meanings that a language learner needs to understand and express. Rather than describe the core of language through traditional concepts of grammar and vocabulary, Wilkins attempted to demonstrate the systems of meanings that lay behind the communicative uses of language. He described two types of meanings: notional categories (concepts such as time, sequence, quantity, location, frequency) and categories of communicative function (requests, denials, offers, complaints). Wilkins later revised and expanded his 1972 document into a book called *Notional Syllabuses* (Wilkins 1976), which had a significant impact on the development of Communicative Language Teaching. The Council of Europe incorporated his semantic/communicative analysis into a set of specifications for a first-level communicative language syllabus. These threshold level specifications (van Ek and Alexander 1980) have had a strong influence on the design of communicative language programs and textbooks in Europe.

The work of the Council of Europe; the writings of Wilkins, Widdowson, Candlin, Christopher Brumfit, Keith Johnson, and other British applied linguists on the theoretical basis for a communicative or functional approach to language teaching; the rapid application of these ideas by textbook writers; and the equally rapid acceptance of these new principles by British language teaching specialists, curriculum development centers, and even governments gave prominence nationally and internationally to what came to be referred to as the Communicative Approach, or simply Communicative Language Teaching. (The terms

notional-functional approach and *functional approach* are also sometimes used.) Although the movement began as a largely British innovation, focusing on alternative conceptions of a syllabus, since the mid-
1970s the scope of Communicative Language Teaching has expanded.
Both American and British proponents now see it as an approach (and
not a method) that aims to (a) make communicative competence the
goal of language teaching and (b) develop procedures for the teaching
of the four language skills that acknowledge the interdependence of
language and communication. Its comprehensiveness thus makes it different in scope and status from any of the other approaches or methods
discussed in this book. There is no single text or authority on it, nor
any single model that is universally accepted as authoritative. For some,
Communicative Language Teaching means little more than an integration of grammatical and functional teaching. Littlewood (1981: 1) states,
"One of the most characteristic features of communicative language
teaching is that it pays systematic attention to functional as well as
structural aspects of language." For others, it means using procedures
where learners work in pairs or groups employing available language
resources in problem-solving tasks. A national primary English syllabus
based on a communicative approach (*Syllabuses for Primary Schools*
1981), for example, defines the focus of the syllabus as the "communicative functions which the forms of the language serve" (p. 5). The
introduction to the same document comments that "communicative purposes may be of many different kinds. What is essential in all of them
is that at least two parties are involved in an interaction or transaction
of some kind where one party has an intention and the other party
expands or reacts to the intention" (p. 5). In her discussion of communicative syllabus design, Yalden (1983) discusses six Communicative
Language Teaching design alternatives, ranging from a model in which
communicative exercises are grafted onto an existing structural syllabus,
to a learner-generated view of syllabus design (e.g., Holec 1980).

Howatt distinguishes between a "strong" and a "weak" version of
Communicative Language Teaching:

There is, in a sense, a 'strong' version of the communicative approach and a
'weak' version. The weak version which has become more or less standard
practice in the last ten years, stresses the importance of providing learners
with opportunities to use their English for communicative purposes and,
characteristically, attempts to integrate such activities into a wider program
of language teaching. . . . The 'strong' version of communicative teaching, on
the other hand, advances the claim that language is acquired through communication, so that it is not merely a question of activating an existing but
inert knowledge of the language, but of stimulating the development of the
language system itself. If the former could be described as 'learning to use'
English, the latter entails 'using English to learn it.' (1984: 279)

Finocchiaro and Brumfit (1983) contrast the major distinctive features of the Audiolingual Method and the Communicative Approach, according to their interpretation:

Audio-lingual

1. Attends to structure and form more than meaning.

2. Demands memorization of structure-based dialogs.

3. Language items are not necessarily contextualized.

4. Language learning is learning structures, sounds, or words.

5. Mastery, or "over-learning" is sought.

6. Drilling is a central technique.

7. Native-speaker-like pronunciation is sought.

8. Grammatical explanation is avoided.

9. Communicative activities only come after a long process of rigid drills and exercises.

10. The use of the student's native language is forbidden.

11. Translation is forbidden at early levels.

12. Reading and writing are deferred till speech is mastered.

13. The target linguistic system will be learned through the overt teaching of the patterns of the system.

14. Linguistic competence is the desired goal.

15. Varieties of language are recognized but not emphasized.

16. The sequence of units is determined solely by principles of linguistic complexity.

Communicative Language Teaching

Meaning is paramount. *need structure, too*

Dialogs, if used, center around communicative functions and are not normally memorized.

Contextualization is a basic premise.

Language learning is learning to communicate. *needs to add this*

Effective communication is sought. *overlearning is important*

Drilling may occur, but peripherally.

Comprehensible pronunciation is sought.

Any device which helps the learners is accepted — varying according to their age, interest, etc.

Attempts to communicate may be encouraged from the very beginning. *⟹ failure ⟹ inferiority*

Judicious use of native language is accepted where feasible.

Translation may be used where students need or benefit from it.

Reading and writing can start from the first day, if desired.

The target linguistic system will be learned best through the process of struggling to communicate.

Communicative competence is the desired goal (i.e. the ability to use the linguistic system effectively and appropriately).

Linguistic variation is a central concept in materials and methodology.

Sequencing is determined by any consideration of content, function, or meaning which maintains interest.

67

17. The teacher controls the learners and prevents them from doing anything that conflicts with the theory.	Teachers help learners in any way that motivates them to work with the language.
18. "Language is habit" so errors must be prevented at all costs.	Language is created by the individual often through trial and error.
19. Accuracy, in terms of formal correctness, is a primary goal.	Fluency and acceptable language is the primary goal: accuracy is judged not in the abstract but in context.
20. Students are expected to interact with the language system, embodied in machines or controlled materials	Students are expected to interact with other people, either in the flesh, through pair and group work, or in their writings.
21. The teacher is expected to specify the language that students are to use.	The teacher cannot know exactly what language the students will use.
22. Intrinsic motivation will spring from an interest in the structure of the language.	Intrinsic motivation will spring from an interest in what is being communicated by the language.

(1983: 91–3)

Apart from being an interesting example of how proponents of Communicative Language Teaching stack the cards in their favor, such a set of contrasts illustrates some of the major differences between communicative approaches and earlier traditions in language teaching. The wide acceptance of the communicative approach and the relatively varied way in which it is interpreted and applied can be attributed to the fact that practitioners from different educational traditions can identify with it, and consequently interpret it in different ways. One of its North American proponents, Savignon (1983), for example, offers as a precedent to CLT a commentary by Montaigne on his learning of Latin through conversation rather than through the customary method of formal analysis and translation. Writes Montaigne, "Without methods, without a book, without grammar or rules, without a whip and without tears, I had learned a Latin as proper as that of my schoolmaster" (Savignon 1983: 47). This antistructural view can be held to represent the language learning version of a more general learning perspective usually referred to as "learning by doing" or "the experience approach" (Hilgard and Bower 1966). This notion of direct rather than delayed practice of communicative acts is central to most CLT interpretations.

The focus on communicative and contextual factors in language use also has an antecedent in the work of the anthropologist Bronislaw Malinowski and his colleague, the linguist John Firth. British applied linguists usually credit Firth with focusing attention on discourse as subject and context for language analysis. Firth also stressed that language needed to be studied in the broader sociocultural context of its use, which included participants, their behavior and beliefs, the objects of linguistic discussion, and word choice. Both Michael Halliday and Dell Hymes, linguists frequently cited by advocates of Communicative Language Teaching, acknowledge primary debts to Malinowski and Firth.

Another frequently cited dimension of CLT, its learner-centered and experience-based view of second language teaching, also has antecedents outside the language teaching tradition per se. An important American national curriculum commission in the 1930s, for example, proposed the adoption of an Experience Curriculum in English. The report of the commission began with the premise that "experience is the best of all schools. . . . The ideal curriculum consists of well-selected experiences" (cited in Applebee 1974: 119). Like those who have recently urged the organization of Communicative Language Teaching around tasks and procedures, the committee tried to suggest "the means for selection and weaving appropriate experiences into a coherent curriculum stretching across the years of school English study" (Applebee 1974: 119). Individual learners were also seen as possessing unique interests, styles, needs, and goals, which should be reflected in the design of methods of instruction. Teachers were encouraged to develop learning materials "on the basis of the particular needs manifested by the class" (Applebee 1974: 150).

Common to all versions of Communicative Language Teaching, however, is a theory of language teaching that starts from a communicative model of language and language use, and that seeks to translate this into a design for an instructional system, for materials, for teacher and learner roles and behaviors, and for classroom activities and techniques. Let us now consider how this is manifested at the levels of approach, design, and procedure.

Approach

Theory of language

The communicative approach in language teaching starts from a theory of language as communication. The goal of language teaching is to develop what Hymes (1972) referred to as "communicative competence." Hymes coined this term in order to contrast a communicative view of language and Chomsky's theory of competence. Chomsky held that linguistic theory is concerned primarily with an ideal speaker-listener in a completely homogeneous speech community, who knows its language perfectly and is unaffected by such grammatically irrelevant conditions as memory limitation, distractions, shifts of attention and interest, and errors (random or characteristic) in applying his knowledge of the language in actual performance. (Chomsky 1965: 3)

For Chomsky, the focus of linguistic theory was to characterize the abstract abilities speakers possess that enable them to produce grammatically correct sentences in a language. Hymes held that such a view of linguistic theory was sterile, that linguistic theory needed to be seen as part of a more general theory incorporating communication and culture. Hymes's theory of communicative competence was a definition of what a speaker needs to know in order to be communicatively competent in a speech community. In Hymes's view, a person who acquires communicative competence acquires both knowledge and ability for language use with respect to

1. whether (and to what degree) something is formally possible;
2. whether (and to what degree) something is feasible in virtue of the means of implementation available;
3. whether (and to what degree) something is appropriate (adequate, happy, successful) in relation to a context in which it is used and evaluated;
4. whether (and to what degree) something is in fact done, actually performed, and what its doing entails.

(Hymes 1972: 281)

This theory of what knowing a language entails offers a much more comprehensive view than Chomsky's view of competence, which deals primarily with abstract grammatical knowledge. Another linguistic theory of communication favored in CLT is Halliday's functional account of language use. "Linguistics . . . is concerned . . . with the description of speech acts or texts, since only through the study of language in use are all the functions of language, and therefore all components of meaning, brought into focus" (Halliday 1970: 145). In a number of influential books and papers, Halliday has elaborated a powerful theory of the functions of language, which complements Hymes's view of communicative competence for many writers on CLT (e.g., Brumfit and Johnson 1979; Savignon 1983). He described (1975: 11–17) seven basic functions that language performs for children learning their first language:

1. the instrumental function: using language to get things;
2. the regulatory function: using language to control the behavior of others;
3. the interactional function: using language to create interaction with others;
4. the personal function: using language to express personal feelings and meanings;

5. the heuristic function: using language to learn and to discover;
6. the imaginative function: using language to create a world of the imagination;
7. the representational function: using language to communicate information.

Learning a second language was similarly viewed by proponents of Communicative Language Teaching as acquiring the linguistic means to perform different kinds of functions.

Another theorist frequently cited for his views on the communicative nature of language is Henry Widdowson. In his book *Teaching Language as Communication* (1978), Widdowson presented a view of the relationship between linguistic systems and their communicative values in text and discourse. He focused on the communicative acts underlying the ability to use language for different purposes. A more recent but related analysis of communicative competence is found in Canale and Swain (1980), in which four dimensions of communicative competence are identified: grammatical competence, sociolinguistic competence, discourse competence, and strategic competence. *Grammatical competence* refers to what Chomsky calls linguistic competence and what Hymes intends by what is "formally possible." It is the domain of grammatical and lexical capacity. *Sociolinguistic competence* refers to an understanding of the social context in which communication takes place, including role relationships, the shared information of the participants, and the communicative purpose for their interaction. *Discourse competence* refers to the interpretation of individual message elements in terms of their interconnectedness and of how meaning is represented in relationship to the entire discourse or text. *Strategic competence* refers to the coping strategies that communicators employ to initiate, terminate, maintain, repair, and redirect communication.

At the level of language theory, Communicative Language Teaching has a rich, if somewhat eclectic, theoretical base. Some of the characteristics of this communicative view of language follow.

1. Language is a system for the expression of meaning.
2. The primary function of language is for interaction and communication.
3. The structure of language reflects its functional and communicative uses.
4. The primary units of language are not merely its grammatical and structural features, but categories of functional and communicative meaning as exemplified in discourse.

Theory of learning

In contrast to the amount that has been written in Communicative Language Teaching literature about communicative dimensions of language, little has been written about learning theory. Neither Brumfit and Johnson (1979) nor Littlewood (1981), for example, offers any discussion of learning theory. Elements of an underlying learning theory can be discerned in some CLT practices, however. One such element might be described as the communication principle: Activities that involve real communication promote learning. A second element is the task principle: Activities in which language is used for carrying out meaningful tasks promote learning (Johnson 1982). A third element is the meaningfulness principle: Language that is meaningful to the learner supports the learning process. Learning activities are consequently selected according to how well they engage the learner in meaningful and authentic language use (rather than merely mechanical practice of language patterns). These principles, we suggest, can be inferred from CLT practices (e.g., Littlewood 1981; Johnson 1982). They address the conditions needed to promote second language learning, rather than the processes of language acquisition.

More recent accounts of Communicative Language Teaching, however, have attempted to describe theories of language learning processes that are compatible with the communicative approach. Savignon (1983) surveys second language acquisition research as a source for learning theories and considers the role of linguistic, social, cognitive, and individual variables in language acquisition. Other theorists (e.g., Stephen Krashen, who is not directly associated with Communicative Language Teaching) have developed theories cited as compatible with the principles of CLT (see Chapter 9). Krashen sees acquisition as the basic process involved in developing language proficiency and distinguishes this process from learning. Acquisition refers to the unconscious development of the target language system as a result of using the language for real communication. Learning is the conscious representation of grammatical knowledge that has resulted from instruction, and it cannot lead to acquisition. It is the acquired system that we call upon to create utterances during spontaneous language use. The learned system can serve only as a monitor of the output of the acquired system. Krashen and other second language acquisition theorists typically stress that language learning comes about through using language communicatively, rather than through practicing language skills.

Johnson (1984) and Littlewood (1984) consider an alternative learning theory that they also see as compatible with CLT—a skill-learning model of learning. According to this theory, the acquisition of communicative competence in a language is an example of skill development. This involves both a cognitive and a behavioral aspect:

The *cognitive* aspect involves the internalisation of plans for creating appropriate behaviour. For language use, these plans derive mainly from the language system – they include grammatical rules, procedures for selecting vocabulary, and social conventions governing speech. The *behavioural* aspect involves the automation of these plans so that they can be converted into fluent performance in real time. This occurs mainly through *practice* in converting plans into performance. (Littlewood 1984: 74)

This theory thus encourages an emphasis on practice as a way of developing communicative skills.

Design

Objectives

Piepho (1981) discusses the following levels of objectives in a communicative approach:

1. an integrative and content level (language as a means of expression)
2. a linguistic and instrumental level (language as a semiotic system and an object of learning);
3. an affective level of interpersonal relationships and conduct (language as a means of expressing values and judgments about oneself and others);
4. a level of individual learning needs (remedial learning based on error analysis);
5. a general educational level of extra-linguistic goals (language learning within the school curriculum).

(Piepho 1981: 8)

These are proposed as general objectives, applicable to any teaching situation. Particular objectives for CLT cannot be defined beyond this level of specification, since such an approach assumes that language teaching will reflect the particular needs of the target learners. These needs may be in the domains of reading, writing, listening, or speaking, each of which can be approached from a communicative perspective. Curriculum or instructional objectives for a particular course would reflect specific aspects of communicative competence according to the learner's proficiency level and communicative needs.

The syllabus

Discussions of the nature of the syllabus have been central in Communicative Language Teaching. We have seen that one of the first syllabus models to be proposed was described as a notional syllabus (Wilkins 1976), which specified the semantic-grammatical categories (e.g., frequency, motion, location) and the categories of communicative function that learners need to express. The Council of Europe expanded and developed this into a syllabus that included descriptions of the objectives of foreign language courses for European adults, the situations in which they might typically need to use a foreign language (e.g., travel, business), the topics they might need to talk about (e.g., personal identification, education, shopping), the functions they needed language for (e.g., describing something, requesting information, expressing agreement and disagreement), the notions made use of in communication (e.g., time, frequency, duration), as well as the vocabulary and grammar needed. The result was published as *Threshold Level English* (van Ek and Alexander 1980) and was an attempt to specify what was needed in order to be able to achieve a reasonable degree of communicative proficiency in a foreign language, including the language items needed to realize this "threshold level."

Discussion of syllabus theory and syllabus models in Communicative Language Teaching has been extensive. Wilkins's original notional syllabus model was soon criticized by British applied linguists as merely replacing one kind of list (e.g., a list of grammar items) with another (a list of notions and functions). It specified products, rather than communicative processes. Widdowson (1979) argued that notional-functional categories provide

only a very partial and imprecise description of certain semantic and pragmatic rules which are used for reference when people interact. They tell us nothing about the procedures people employ in the application of these rules when they are actually engaged in communicative activity. If we are to adopt a communicative approach to teaching which takes as its primary purpose the development of the ability to do things with language, then it is discourse which must be at the center of our attention. (Widdowson 1979: 254)

There are at present several proposals and models for what a syllabus might look like in Communicative Language Teaching. Yalden (1983) describes the major current communicative syllabus types. We summarize below a modified version of Yalden's classification of communicative syllabus types, with reference sources to each model:

Type	*Reference*
1. structures plus functions	Wilkins (1976)
2. functional spiral around a structural core	Brumfit (1980)
3. structural, functional, instrumental	Allen (1980)
4. functional	Jupp and Hodlin (1975)
5. notional	Wilkins (1976)
6. interactional	Widdowson (1979)
7. task-based	Prabhu (1983)
8. learner generated	Candlin (1976), Henner-Stanchina and Riley (1978)

There is extensive documentation of attempts to create syllabus and proto-syllabus designs of types 1–5. A current interest is in syllabus designs of types 6–8, although specifications of organizing principles for interactional, task-based, and learner-generated syllabuses have been only partially accomplished. Descriptions of interactional strategies have been given, for example, for interactions of teacher and student (Sinclair and Coulthard 1975) and doctor and patient (Candlin, Bruton, and Leather 1974). Although interesting, these descriptions have restricted the field of inquiry to two-person interactions in which there exist reasonably rigid and acknowledged superordinate to subordinate role relationships.

Some designers of communicative syllabuses have also looked to task specification and task organization as the appropriate criteria for syllabus design.

The only form of syllabus which is compatible with and can support communicational teaching seems to be a purely procedural one—which lists in more or less detail, the types of tasks to be attempted in the classroom and suggests an order of complexity for tasks of the same kind. (Prabhu 1983: 4)

An example of such a model that has been implemented nationally is the Malaysian communicational syllabus (English Language Syllabus in Malaysian Schools 1975) – a syllabus for the teaching of English at the upper secondary level in Malaysia. This was one of the first attempts to organize Communicative Language Teaching around a specification of communication tasks. In the organizational schema three broad communicative objectives are broken down into twenty-four more specific objectives determined on the basis of needs analysis. These objectives are organized into learning areas, for each of which are specified a number of outcome goals or products. A product is defined as a piece of comprehensible information, written, spoken, or presented in a nonlinguistic form. "A letter is a product, and so is an instruction, a message, a report or a map or graph produced through information gleaned through language" (English Language Syllabus 1975: 5). The products, then, result from successful completion of tasks. For example, the product called "relaying a message to others" can be broken into a number of tasks, such as (a) understanding the message, (b) asking questions to clear any doubts (c) asking questions to gather more information, (d) taking notes, (e) arranging the notes in a logical manner for presentation, and (f) orally presenting the message. For each product a number of proposed situations are suggested. These situations consist of a set of specifications for learner interactions, the stimuli, communicative context, participants, desired outcomes, and constraints. These situations (and others constructed by individual teachers) constitute the means by which learner interaction and communicative skills are realized.

As discussion of syllabus models continues in the CLT literature, some have argued that the syllabus concept be abolished altogether in its accepted forms, arguing that only learners can be fully aware of their own needs, communicational resources, and desired learning pace and path, and that each learner must create a personal, albeit implicit, syllabus as part of learning. Others lean more toward the model proposed by Brumfit (1980), which favors a grammatically based syllabus around which notions, functions, and communicational activities are grouped.

Types of learning and teaching activities

The range of exercise types and activities compatible with a communicative approach is unlimited, provided that such exercises enable learners to attain the communicative objectives of the curriculum, engage learners in communication, and require the use of such communicative processes as information sharing, negotiation of meaning, and interaction. Classroom activities are often designed to focus on completing tasks that are mediated through language or involve negotiation of information and information sharing.

These attempts take many forms. Wright (1976) achieves it by showing out-of-focus slides which the students attempt to identify. Byrne (1978) provides incomplete plans and diagrams which students have to complete by asking for information. Allwright (1977) places a screen between students and gets one to place objects in a certain pattern: this pattern is then communicated to students behind the screen. Geddes and Sturtridge (1979) develop "jigsaw" listening in which students listen to different taped materials and then communicate their content to others in the class. Most of these techniques operate by providing information to some and withholding it from others. (Johnson 1982: 151)

Littlewood (1981) distinguishes between "functional communication activities" and "social interaction activities" as major activity types in Communicative Language Teaching. Functional communication activities include such tasks as learners comparing sets of pictures and noting similarities and differences; working out a likely sequence of events in a set of pictures; discovering missing features in a map or picture; one learner communicating behind a screen to another learner and giving instructions on how to draw a picture or shape, or how to complete a map; following directions; and solving problems from shared clues. Social interaction activities include conversation and discussion sessions, dialogues and role plays, simulations, skits, improvisations, and debates.

Learner roles

The emphasis in Communicative Language Teaching on the processes of communication, rather than mastery of language forms, leads to different roles for learners from those found in more traditional second language classrooms. Breen and Candlin describe the learner's role within CLT in the following terms:

The role of learner as negotiator—between the self, the learning process, and the object of learning—emerges from and interacts with the role of joint nego-tiator within the group and within the classroom procedures and activities which the group undertakes. The implication for the learner is that he should contribute as much as he gains, and thereby learn in an interdependent way. (1980: 110)

There is thus an acknowledgment, in some accounts of CLT, that learners bring preconceptions of what teaching and learning should be like. These constitute a "set" for learning, which when unrealized can lead to learner confusion and resentment (Henner-Stanchina and Riley 1978). Often there is no text, grammar rules are not presented, classroom arrangement is nonstandard, students are expected to interact primarily with each other rather than with the teacher, and correction of errors may be absent or infrequent. The cooperative (rather than individualistic) ap-proach to learning stressed in CLT may likewise be unfamiliar to learn-ers. CLT methodologists consequently recommend that learners learn to see that failed communication is a joint responsibility and not the fault of speaker or listener. Similarly, successful communication is an accomplishment jointly achieved and acknowledged.

Teacher roles

Several roles are assumed for teachers in Communicative Language Teaching, the importance of particular roles being determined by the view of CLT adopted. Breen and Candlin describe teacher roles in the following terms:

The teacher has two main roles: the first role is to facilitate the communica-tion process between all participants in the classroom, and between these participants and the various activities and texts. The second role is to act as an independent participant within the learning-teaching group. The latter role is closely related to the objectives of the first role and arises from it. These roles imply a set of secondary roles for the teacher; first, as an organizer of resources and as a resource himself, second as a guide within the classroom procedures and activities. . . . A third role for the teacher is that of researcher and learner, with much to contribute in terms of appropriate knowledge and abilities, actual and observed experience of the nature of learning and organi-zational capacities. (1980: 99)

Other roles assumed for teachers are needs analyst, counselor, and group process manager.

NEEDS ANALYST

The CLT teacher assumes a responsibility for determining and responding to learner language needs. This may be done informally and personally through one-to-one sessions with students, in which the teacher talks through such issues as the student's perception of his or her learning style, learning assets, and learning goals. It may be done formally through administering a needs assessment instrument, such as those exemplified in Savignon (1983). Typically, such formal assessments contain items that attempt to determine an individual's motivation for studying the language. For example, students might respond on a 5-point scale (*strongly agree* to *strongly disagree*) to statements like the following.

I want to study English because...
1. I think it will someday be useful in getting a good job.
2. it will help me better understand English-speaking people and their way of life.
3. one needs a good knowledge of English to gain other people's respect.
4. it will allow me to meet and converse with interesting people.
5. I need it for my job.
6. it will enable me to think and behave like English-speaking people.

On the basis of such needs assessments, teachers are expected to plan group and individual instruction that responds to the learners' needs.

COUNSELOR

Another role assumed by several CLT approaches is that of counselor, similar to the way this role is defined in Community Language Learning. In this role, the teacher-counselor is expected to exemplify an effective communicator seeking to maximize the meshing of speaker intention and hearer interpretation, through the use of paraphrase, confirmation, and feedback.

GROUP PROCESS MANAGER

CLT procedures often require teachers to acquire less teacher-centered classroom management skills. It is the teacher's responsibility to organize the classroom as a setting for communication and communicative activities. Guidelines for classroom practice (e.g., Littlewood 1981; Finocchiaro and Brumfit 1983) suggest that during an activity the teacher monitors, encourages, and suppresses the inclination to supply gaps in lexis, grammar, and strategy but notes such gaps for later commentary and communicative practice. At the conclusion of group activities, the teacher leads in the debriefing of the activity, pointing out alternatives and extensions and assisting groups in self-correction discussion. Critics have pointed out, however, that non-native teachers may feel less than comfortable about such procedures without special training.

The focus on fluency and comprehensibility in Communicative Language Teaching may cause anxiety among teachers accustomed to seeing error suppression and correction as the major instructional responsibility, and who see their primary function as preparing learners to take standardized or other kinds of tests. A continuing teacher concern has been the possible deleterious effect in pair or group work of imperfect modeling and student error. Although this issue is far from resolved, it is interesting to note that recent research findings suggest that "data contradicts the notion that other learners are not good conversational partners because they can't provide accurate input when it is solicited" (Porter 1983).

The role of instructional materials

A wide variety of materials have been used to support communicative approaches to language teaching. Unlike some contemporary methodologies, such as Community Language Learning, practitioners of Communicative Language Teaching view materials as a way of influencing the quality of classroom interaction and language use. Materials thus have the primary role of promoting communicative language use. We will consider three kinds of materials currently used in CLT and label these text-based, task-based, and realia.

TEXT-BASED MATERIALS

There are numerous textbooks designed to direct and support Communicative Language Teaching. Their tables of contents sometimes suggest a kind of grading and sequencing of language practice not unlike those found in structurally organized texts. Some of these are in fact written around a largely structural syllabus, with slight reformatting to justify their claims to be based on a communicative approach. Others, however, look very different from previous language teaching texts. Morrow and Johnson's *Communicate* (1979), for example, has none of the usual dialogues, drills, or sentence patterns and uses visual cues, taped cues, pictures, and sentence fragments to initiate conversation. Watcyn-Jones's *Pair Work* (1981) consists of two different texts for pair work, each containing different information needed to enact role plays and carry out other pair activities. Texts written to support the Malaysian *English Language Syllabus* (1975) likewise represent a departure from traditional textbook modes. A typical lesson consists of a theme (e.g., relaying information), a task analysis for thematic development (e.g., understanding the message, asking questions to obtain clarification, asking for more information, taking notes, ordering and presenting information), a practice situation description (e.g., "A caller asks to see your manager. He does not have an appointment. Gather the necessary information from him and relay the message to your manager."), a stimulus presentation (in the preceding case, the beginning of an office conversation scripted and on tape), comprehension questions (e.g., "Why is the caller in the office?"), and paraphrase exercises.

TASK-BASED MATERIALS

A variety of games, role plays, simulations, and task-based communication activities have been prepared to support Communicative Language Teaching classes. These typically are in the form of one-of-a-kind items: exercise handbooks, cue cards, activity cards, pair-communication practice materials, and student-interaction practice booklets. In pair-communication materials, there are typically two sets of material for a pair of students, each set containing different kinds of information. Sometimes the information is complementary, and partners must fit their respective parts of the "jigsaw" into a composite whole. Others assume different role relationships for the partners (e.g., an interviewer and an interviewee). Still others provide drills and practice material in interactional formats.

REALIA

Many proponents of Communicative Language Teaching have advocated the use of "authentic," "from-life" materials in the classroom. These might include language-based realia, such as signs, magazines, advertisements, and newspapers, or graphic and visual sources around which communicative activities can be built, such as maps, pictures, symbols, graphs, and charts. Different kinds of objects can be used to support communicative exercises, such as a plastic model to assemble from directions.

Procedure

Because communicative principles can be applied to the teaching of any skill, at any level, and because of the wide variety of classroom activities and exercise types discussed in the literature on Communicative Language Teaching, description of typical classroom procedures used in a lesson based on CLT principles is not feasible. Savignon (1983) discusses techniques and classroom management procedures associated with a number of CLT classroom procedures (e.g., group activities, language games, role plays), but neither these activities nor the ways in which they are used are exclusive to CLT classrooms. Finocchiaro and Brumfit offer a lesson outline for teaching the function "making a suggestion" for learners in the beginning level of a secondary school program that suggests that CLT procedures are evolutionary rather than revolutionary:

1. Presentation of a brief dialog or several mini-dialogs, preceded by a motivation (relating the dialog situation(s) to the learners' probable community experiences) and a discussion of the function and situation—people, roles, setting, topic, and the informality or formality of the language which the function and situation demand. (At beginning levels, where all the learners understand the same native language, the motivation can well be given in their native tongue).
2. Oral practice of each utterance of the dialog segment to be presented that day (entire class repetition, half-class, groups, individuals) generally preceded by your model. If mini-dialogs are used, engage in similar practice.
3. Questions and answers based on the dialog topic(s) and situation itself. (Inverted wh, or or questions).
4. Questions and answers related to the students' personal experiences but centered around the dialog theme.
5. Study one of the basic communicative expressions in the dialog or one of the structures which exemplify the function. You will wish to give several additional examples of the communicative use of the expression or structure with familiar vocabulary in unambiguous utterances or mini-dialogs (using pictures, simple real objects, or dramatization) to clarify the meaning of the expression or structure....
6. Learner discovery of generalizations or rules underlying the functional expression or structure. This should include at least four points: its oral and written forms (the elements of which it is composed, e.g. "How about + verb + ing?"); its position in the utterance; its formality or informality in the utterance; and in the case of a structure, its grammatical function and meaning....
7. Oral recognition, interpretative activities (two to five depending on the learning level, the language knowledge of the students, and related factors).
8. Oral production activities—proceeding from guided to freer communication activities.
9. Copying of the dialogs or mini-dialogs or modules if they are not in the class text.
10. Sampling of the written homework assignment, if given.
11. Evaluation of learning (oral only), e.g. "How would you ask your friend to _____? And how would you ask me to _____?"

(Finocchiaro and Brumfit 1983: 107–8)

Such procedures clearly have much in common with those observed in classes taught according to Structural-Situational and Audiolingual principles. Traditional procedures are not rejected but are reinterpreted and extended. A similar conservatism is found in many "orthodox" CLT texts, such as Alexander's *Mainline Beginners* (1978). Although each unit has an ostensibly functional focus, new teaching points are introduced with dialogues, followed by controlled practice of the main grammatical patterns. The teaching points are then contextualized through situational practice. This serves as an introduction to a freer practice activity, such as a role play or improvisation. Similar techniques are used in another popular textbook, *Starting Strategies* (Abbs and Freebairn 1977). Teaching points are introduced in dialogue form, grammatical items are isolated for controlled practice, and then freer activities are provided. Pair and group work is suggested to encourage students to use and practice functions and forms. The methodological procedures underlying these texts reflects a sequence of activities represented in Littlewood (1981, p. 86) as follows:

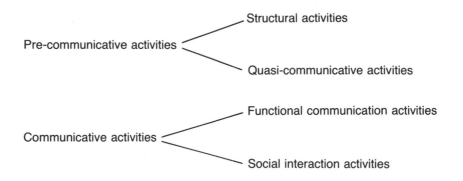

Savignon (1972, 1983), however, rejects the notion that learners must first gain control over individual skills (pronunciation, grammar, vocabulary) before applying them in communicative tasks; she advocates providing communicative practice from the start of instruction. How to implement CLT principles at the level of classroom procedures thus remains central to discussions of the communicative approach. How can the range of communicative activities and procedures be defined, and how can the teacher determine a mix and timing of activities that best meets the needs of a particular learner or group of learners? These fundamental questions cannot be answered by proposing further taxonomies and classifications, but require systematic investigation of the use of different kinds of activities and procedures in L2 classrooms (see Chapter 11).

Conclusion

Communicative Language Teaching is best considered an approach rather than a method. Thus although a reasonable degree of theoretical consistency can be discerned at the levels of language and learning theory, at the levels of design and procedure there is much greater room for individual interpretation and variation than most methods permit. It could be that one version among the various proposals for syllabus models, exercise types, and classroom activities may gain wider approval in the future, giving Communicative Language Teaching a status similar to other teaching methods. On the other hand, divergent interpretations might lead to homogeneous subgroups.

Communicative Language Teaching appeared at a time when British language teaching was ready for a paradigm shift. Situational Language Teaching was no longer felt to reflect a methodology appropriate for the seventies and beyond. CLT appealed to those who sought a more humanistic approach to teaching, one in which the interactive processes of communication received priority. The rapid adoption and implementation of the communicative approach also resulted from the fact that it quickly assumed the status of orthodoxy in British language teaching circles, receiving the sanction and support of leading British applied linguists, language specialists, publishers, as well as institutions, such as the British Council (Richards 1985).

Now that the initial wave of enthusiasm has passed, however, some of the claims of CLT are being looked at more critically (Swan 1985). The adoption of a communicative approach raises important issues for teacher training, materials development, and testing and evaluation. Questions that have been raised include whether a communicative approach can be applied at all levels in a language program, whether it is equally suited to ESL and EFL situations, whether it requires existing grammar-based syllabuses to be abandoned or merely revised, how such an approach can be evaluated, how suitable it is for non-native teachers, and how it can be adopted in situations where students must continue to take grammar-based tests. These kinds of questions will doubtless require attention if the communicative movement in language teaching continues to gain momentum in the future.

Bibliography

Abbs, B. A., and I. Freebairn. 1977. *Starting Strategies*. London: Longman.
Alexander, L. G. 1978. *Mainline Beginners*. London: Longman.
Allen, J. P. B. 1980. A three-level curriculum model for second language edu-

cation. Mimeo: Modern Language Center, Ontario Institute for Studies in Education.

Allwright, R. L. 1977. Language learning through communication practice. *ELT Documents* 76(3). London: British Council.

Applebee, A. N. 1974. *Tradition and Reform in the Teaching of English: A History.* Urbana, Ill.: National Council of Teachers of English.

Austin, J. L. 1962. *How to Do Things with Words.* Oxford: Clarendon Press.

Breen, M., and C. N. Candlin. 1980. The essentials of a communicative curriculum in language teaching. *Applied Linguistics* 1(2): 89–112.

Brumfit, C. 1980. From defining to designing: communicative specifications versus communicative methodology in foreign language teaching. In K. Muller (ed.), *The Foreign Language Syllabus and Communicative Approaches to Teaching: Proceedings of a European-American Seminar.* Special issue of *Studies in Second Language Acquisition,* 3(1): 1–9.

Brumfit, C. J., and K. Johnson (eds.). 1979. *The Communicative Approach to Language Teaching.* Oxford: Oxford University Press.

Byrne, D. 1978. *Materials for Language Teaching: Interaction Packages.* London: Modern English Publications.

Canale, M., and M. Swain. 1980. Theoretical bases of communicative approaches to second language teaching and testing. *Applied Linguistics* 1(1): 1–47.

Candlin, C. N. 1976. Communicative language teaching and the debt to pragmatics. In C. Rameh (ed.), *Georgetown University Roundtable 1976.* Washington, D.C.: Georgetown University Press.

Candlin, C. N., C. J. Bruton, and J. H. Leather. 1974. Doctor–patient communication skills. Mimeo, University of Lancaster.

Chomsky, N. 1957. *Syntactic Structures.* The Hague: Mouton.

Chomsky, N. 1965. *Aspects of the Theory of Syntax.* Boston: MIT Press.

English Language Syllabus in Malaysian Schools, Tingkatan 4–5. 1975. Kuala Lumpur: Dewan Bahasa Dan Pustaka.

Finocchiaro, M., and C. Brumfit. 1983. *The Functional-Notional Approach: From Theory to Practice.* New York: Oxford University Press.

Firth, J. R. 1957. *Papers in Linguistics: 1934–1951.* London: Oxford University Press.

Geddes, M., and G. Sturtridge. 1979. *Listening Links.* London: Heinemann.

Gumperz, J. J., and D. Hymes (eds.). 1972. *Directions in Sociolinguistics: The Ethnography of Communication.* New York: Holt, Rinehart and Winston.

Halliday, M. A. K. 1970. Language structure and language function. In J. Lyons (ed.), *New Horizons in Linguistics,* pp. 140–65. Harmondsworth: Penguin.

Halliday, M. A. K. 1973. *Explorations in the Functions of Language.* London: Edward Arnold.

Halliday, M. A. K. 1975. *Learning How to Mean: Explorations in the Development of Language.* London: Edward Arnold.

Halliday, M. A. K. 1978. *Language as Social Semiotic.* London: Edward Arnold.

Henner-Stanchina, C., and P. Riley. 1978. Aspects of autonomous learning. In *ELT Documents 103: Individualization in Language Learning,* pp. 75–97. London: British Council.

Hilgard, E. R., and G. H. Bower. 1966. *Theories of Learning*. New York: Appleton-Century-Crofts.

Holec, H. 1980. *Autonomy and Foreign Language Learning*. Strasbourg: Council of Europe.

Howatt, A. P. R. 1984. *A History of English Language Teaching*. Oxford: Oxford University Press.

Hymes, D. 1972. On communicative competence. In J. B. Pride and J. Holmes (eds.), *Sociolinguistics*, pp. 269–93. Harmondsworth: Penguin.

Johnson, 1982. *Communicative Syllabus Design and Methodology*. Oxford: Pergamon.

Johnson, 1984. Skill psychology and communicative methodology. Paper presented at the RELC seminar, Singapore.

Jupp, T. C., and S. Hodlin. 1975. *Industrial English: An Example of Theory and Practice in Functional Language Teaching*. London: Heinemann.

Littlewood, W. 1981. *Communicative Language Teaching*. Cambridge: Cambridge University Press.

Littlewood, W. 1984. *Foreign and Second Language Learning: Language Acquisition Research and Its Implications for the Classroom*. Cambridge: Cambridge University Press.

Morrow, K., and K. Johnson. 1979. *Communicate*. Cambridge: Cambridge University Press.

Munby, J. 1978. *Communicative Syllabus Design*. Cambridge: Cambridge University Press.

Piepho, H.-E. 1981. Establishing objectives in the teaching of English. In C. Candlin (ed.), *The Communicative Teaching of English: Principles and an Exercise Typology*. London: Longman.

Porter, P. A. 1983. Variations in the conversations of adult learners of English as a function of the proficiency level of the participants. Ph.D. dissertation, Stanford University.

Prabhu, N. 1983. Procedural syllabuses. Paper presented at the RELC Seminar, Singapore.

Richards, J. C. 1985. The secret life of methods. In Richards, *The Context of Language Teaching*, pp. 32–45. Cambridge: Cambridge University Press.

Savignon, S. 1972. Teaching for communicative competence: a research report. *Audiovisual Language Journal* 10(3): 153–62.

Savignon, S. 1983. *Communicative Competence: Theory and Classroom Practice*. Reading, Mass.: Addison-Wesley.

Searle, J. R. 1969. *Speech Acts: An Essay in the Philosophy of Language*. Cambridge: Cambridge University Press.

Sinclair, J. McH., and R. M. Coulthard. 1975. *Towards an Analysis of Discourse*. Oxford: Oxford University Press.

Swan, M. 1985. A critical look at the communicative approach. *English Language Teaching Journal*, pt. 1, 39(1): 2–12.

Syllabuses for Primary Schools. 1981. Hong Kong: Curriculum Development Committee Hong Kong.

Van Ek, J. A. 1975. *The Threshold Level in a European Unit/Credit System for Modern Language Teaching by Adults*. Systems Development in Adult Language Learning. Strasbourg: Council of Europe.

Van Ek, J., and L. G. Alexander. 1980. *Threshold Level English*. Oxford: Pergamon.

Watcyn-Jones, P. 1981. *Pair Work*. Harmondsworth: Penguin Books.

Widdowson, H. G. 1972. The teaching of English as communication. *English Language Teaching* 27(1): 15–18.

Widdowson, H. G. 1978. *Teaching Language as Communication*. Oxford: Oxford University Press.

Widdowson, H. G. 1979. The communicative approach and its applications. In H. G. Widdowson, *Explorations in Applied Linguistics*. Oxford: Oxford University Press.

Wilkins, D. A. 1972. The linguistic and situational content of the common core in a unit/credit system. Ms. Strasbourg: Council of Europe.

Wilkins, D. A. 1976. *Notional Syllabuses*. Oxford: Oxford University Press.

Wilkins, D. A. 1979. Notional syllabuses and the concept of a minimum adequate grammar. In C. J. Brumfit and K. Johnson (eds.), *The Communicative Approach to Language Teaching*. Oxford: Oxford University Press.

Wright, A. 1976. *Visual Material for the Language Teacher*. London: Longman.

Yalden, J. 1983. *The Communicative Syllabus: Evolution, Design and Implementation*. Oxford: Pergamon.

6 Total Physical Response

Background

Total Physical Response (TPR) is a language teaching method built around the coordination of speech and action; it attempts to teach language through physical (motor) activity. Developed by James Asher, a professor of psychology at San Jose State University, California, it draws on several traditions, including developmental psychology, learning theory, and humanistic pedagogy, as well as on language teaching procedures proposed by Harold and Dorothy Palmer in 1925. Let us briefly consider these precedents to Total Physical Response.

Total Physical Response is linked to the "trace theory" of memory in psychology (e.g., Katona 1940), which holds that the more often or the more intensively a memory connection is traced, the stronger the memory association will be and the more likely it will be recalled. Retracing can be done verbally (e.g., by rote repetition) and/or in association with motor activity. Combined tracing activities, such as verbal rehearsal accompanied by motor activity, hence increase the probability of successful recall.

In a developmental sense, Asher sees successful adult second language learning as a parallel process to child first language acquisition. He claims that speech directed to young children consists primarily of commands, which children respond to physically before they begin to produce verbal responses. Asher feels adults should recapitulate the processes by which children acquire their mother tongue.

Asher shares with the school of humanistic psychology a concern for the role of affective (emotional) factors in language learning. A method that is undemanding in terms of linguistic production and that involves gamelike movements reduces learner stress, he believes, and creates a positive mood in the learner, which facilitates learning.

Asher's emphasis on developing comprehension skills before the learner is taught to speak links him to a movement in foreign language teaching sometimes referred to as the Comprehension Approach (Winitz 1981). This refers to several different comprehension-based language teaching proposals, which share the belief that (a) comprehension abilities precede productive skills in learning a language; (b) the teaching of speaking should be delayed until comprehension skills are established; (c) skills acquired through listening transfer to other skills; (d) teaching should emphasize meaning rather than form; and (e) teaching should minimize learner stress.

The emphasis on comprehension and the use of physical actions to teach a foreign language at an introductory level has a long tradition in language teaching. We saw in Chapter 1 that in the nineteenth century Gouin had advocated a situationally based teaching strategy in which a chain of action verbs served as the basis for introducing and practicing new language items. Palmer experimented with an action-based teaching strategy in his book *English Through Actions* (first published in Tokyo in 1925 and ultimately reissued as Palmer and Palmer in 1959), which claimed that "no method of teaching foreign speech is likely to be economical or successful which does not include in the first period a very considerable proportion of that type of classroom work which consists of the carrying out by the pupil of orders issued by the teacher" (Palmer and Palmer 1959: 39).

Approach

Theory of language

Asher does not directly discuss the nature of language or how languages are organized. However, the labeling and ordering of TPR classroom drills seem to be built on assumptions that owe much to structuralist or grammar-based views of language. Asher states that "most of the grammatical structure of the target language and hundreds of vocabulary items can be learned from the skillful use of the imperative by the instructor" (1977: 4). He views the verb, and particularly the verb in the imperative, as the central linguistic motif around which language use and learning are organized.

Asher sees language as being composed of abstractions and nonabstractions, with nonabstractions being most specifically represented by concrete nouns and imperative verbs. He believes that learners can acquire a "detailed cognitive map" as well as "the grammatical structure of a language" without recourse to abstractions.

Abstractions should be delayed until students have internalized a detailed cognitive map of the target language. Abstractions are not necessary for people to decode the grammatical structure of a language. Once students have internalized the code, abstractions can be introduced and explained in the target language. (Asher 1977: 11–12)

This is an interesting claim about language but one that is insufficiently detailed to test. For example, are tense, aspect, articles, and so forth, abstractions, and if so, what sort of "detailed cognitive map" could be constructed without them?

Despite Asher's belief in the central role of comprehension in language learning, he does not elaborate on the relation between comprehension, production, and communication (he has no theory of speech acts or their equivalents, for example), although in advanced TPR lessons imperatives are used to initiate different speech acts, such as requests ("John, ask Mary to walk to the door"), and apologies ("Ned, tell Jack you're sorry").

Asher also refers in passing to the fact that language can be internalized as wholes or chunks, rather than as single lexical items, and, as such, links are possible to more theoretical proposals of this kind (e.g., Miller, Galanter, and Pribram 1960), as well as to work on the role of prefabricated patterns in language learning and language use (e.g., Yorio 1980). Asher does not elaborate on his view of chunking, however, nor on other aspects of the theory of language underlying Total Physical Response. We have only clues to what a more fully developed language theory might resemble when spelled out by Asher and his supporters.

Theory of learning

Asher's language learning theories are reminiscent of the views of other behavioral psychologists. For example, the psychologist Arthur Jensen proposed a seven-stage model to describe the development of verbal learning in children. The first stage he calls Sv-R type learning, which the educational psychologist John DeCecco interprets as follows:

In Jensen's notation, Sv refers to a verbal stimulus—a syllable, a word, a phrase, and so on. R refers to the physical movements the child makes in response to the verbal stimulus (or Sv). The movement may involve touching, grasping, or otherwise manipulating some object. For example, mother may tell Percival (age 1) to get the ball, and Percival, distinguishing the sound "ball" from the clatter of other household noises, responds by fetching the ball and bringing it to his mother. Ball is the Sv (verbal stimulus), and Percival's action is the response. At Percival's age, children respond to words about four times faster than they respond to other sounds in their environment. It is not clear why this is so, but it is possible that the reinforcing effects of making proper responses to verbal stimuli are sufficiently strong to cause a rapid development of this behavior. Sv-R learning represents, then, the simplest form of verbal behavior. (DeCecco 1968: 329)

This is a very similar position to Asher's view of child language acquisition. Although learning psychologists such as Jensen have since abandoned such simple stimulus-response models of language acquisition and development, and although linguists have rejected them as incapable of accounting for the fundamental features of language learning and use (see Chapter 4), Asher still sees a stimulus-response view as providing the learning theory underlying language teaching pedagogy. In addition,

Asher has elaborated an account of what he feels facilitates or inhibits foreign language learning. For this dimension of his learning theory he draws on three rather influential learning hypotheses:

1. There exists a specific innate bio-program for language learning, which defines an optimal path for first and second language development.
2. Brain lateralization defines different learning functions in the left- and right-brain hemispheres.
3. Stress (an affective filter) intervenes between the act of learning and what is to be learned; the lower the stress, the greater the learning.

Let us consider how Asher views each of these in turn.

1. THE BIO-PROGRAM

Asher's Total Physical Response is a "Natural Method" (see Chapter 1), inasmuch as Asher sees first and second language learning as parallel processes. Second language teaching and learning should reflect the naturalistic processes of first language learning. Asher sees three processes as central. (a) Children develop listening competence before they develop the ability to speak. At the early stages of first language acquisition they can understand complex utterances that they cannot spontaneously produce or imitate. Asher speculates that during this period of listening, the learner may be making a mental "blueprint" of the language that will make it possible to produce spoken language later. (b) Children's ability in listening comprehension is acquired because children are required to respond physically to spoken language in the form of parental commands. (c) Once a foundation in listening comprehension has been established, speech evolves naturally and effortlessly out of it. As we noted earlier, these principles are held by proponents of a number of other method proposals and are referred to collectively as a Comprehension Approach.

Parallel to the processes of first language learning, the foreign language learner should first internalize a "cognitive map" of the target language through listening exercises. Listening should be accompanied by physical movement. Speech and other productive skills should come later. The speech-production mechanisms will begin to function spontaneously when the basic foundations of language are established through listening training. Asher bases these assumptions on his belief in the existence in the human brain of a bio-program for language, which defines an optimal order for first and second language learning.

A reasonable hypothesis is that the brain and nervous system are biologically programmed to acquire language . . . in a particular sequence and in a particular mode. The sequence is listening before speaking and the mode is to synchronize language with the individual's body. (Asher 1977: 4)

90

2. BRAIN LATERALIZATION

Asher sees Total Physical Response as directed to right-brain learning, whereas most second language teaching methods are directed to left-brain learning. Asher refers to neurological studies of the brains of cats and studies of an epileptic boy whose corpus callosum was surgically divided. Asher interprets these as demonstrating that the brain is divided into hemispheres according to function, with language activities centralized in the right hemisphere. Drawing on work by Jean Piaget, Asher holds that the child language learner acquires language through motor movement – a right-hemisphere activity. Right-hemisphere activities must occur before the left hemisphere can process language for production.

Similarly, the adult should proceed to language mastery through right-hemisphere motor activities, while the left hemisphere watches and learns. When a sufficient amount of right-hemisphere learning has taken place, the left hemisphere will be triggered to produce language and to initiate other, more abstract language processes.

3. REDUCTION OF STRESS

An important condition for successful language learning is the absence of stress. First language acquisition takes place in a stress-free environment, according to Asher, whereas the adult language learning environment often causes considerable stress and anxiety. The key to stress-free learning is to tap into the natural bio-program for language development and thus to recapture the relaxed and pleasurable experiences that accompany first language learning. By focusing on meaning interpreted through movement, rather than on language forms studied in the abstract, the learner is said to be liberated from self-conscious and stressful situations and is able to devote full energy to learning.

Design

Objectives

The general objectives of Total Physical Response are to teach oral proficiency at a beginning level. Comprehension is a means to an end, and the ultimate aim is to teach basic speaking skills. A TPR course aims to produce learners who are capable of an uninhibited communication that is intelligible to a native speaker. Specific instructional objectives are not elaborated, for these will depend on the particular needs of the learners. Whatever goals are set, however, must be attainable through the use of action-based drills in the imperative form.

The syllabus

The type of syllabus Asher uses can be inferred from an analysis of the exercise types employed in TPR classes. This analysis reveals the use of a sentence-based syllabus, with grammatical and lexical criteria being primary in selecting teaching items. Unlike methods that operate from a grammar-based or structural view of the core elements of language, Total Physical Response requires initial attention to meaning rather than to the form of items. Grammar is thus taught inductively. Grammatical features and vocabulary items are selected not according to their frequency of need or use in target language situations, but according to the situations in which they can be used in the classroom and the ease with which they can be learned.

> The criterion for including a vocabulary item or grammatical feature at a particular point in training is ease of assimilation by students. If an item is not learned rapidly, this means that the students are not ready for that item. Withdraw it and try again at a future time in the training program. (Asher 1977: 42)

Asher also suggests that a fixed number of items be introduced at a time, to facilitate ease of differentiation and assimilation. "In an hour, it is possible for students to assimilate 12 to 36 new lexical items depending upon the size of the group and the stage of training" (Asher 1977: 42).

Asher sees a need for attention to both the global meaning of language as well as to the finer details of its organization.

> The movement of the body seems to be a powerful mediator for the understanding, organization and storage of macro-details of linguistic input. Language can be internalized in chunks, but alternative strategies must be developed for fine-tuning to macro-details. (Asher, Kusudo, and de la Torre 1974: 28)

A course designed around Total Physical Response principles, however, would not be expected to follow a TPR syllabus exclusively.

> We are not advocating only one strategy of learning. Even if the imperative is the major or minor format of training, variety is critical for maintaining continued student interest. The imperative is a powerful facilitator of learning, but it should be used in combination with many other techniques. The optimal combination will vary from instructor to instructor and class to class. (Asher 1977: 28)

Types of learning and teaching activities

Imperative drills are the major classroom activity in Total Physical Response. They are typically used to elicit physical actions and activity on the part of the learners. Conversational dialogues are delayed until after about 120 hours of instruction. Asher's rationale for this is that "everyday conversations are highly abstract and disconnected; therefore to understand them requires a rather advanced internalization of the target language" (1977: 95). Other class activities include role plays and slide presentations. Role plays center on everyday situations, such as at the restaurant, supermarket, or gas station. The slide presentations are used to provide a visual center for teacher narration, which is followed by commands, and for questions to students, such as "Which person in the picture is the salesperson?". Reading and writing activities may also be employed to further consolidate structures and vocabulary, and as follow-ups to oral imperative drills.

Learner roles

Learners in Total Physical Response have the primary roles of listener and performer. They listen attentively and respond physically to commands given by the teacher. Learners are required to respond both individually and collectively. Learners have little influence over the content of learning, since content is determined by the teacher, who must follow the imperative-based format for lessons. Learners are also expected to recognize and respond to novel combinations of previously taught items:

Novel utterances are recombinations of constituents you have used directly in training. For instance, you directed students with 'Walk to the table!' and 'Sit on the chair!'. These are familiar to students since they have practiced responding to them. Now, will a student understand if you surprise the individual with an unfamiliar utterance that you created by recombining familiar elements (e.g. 'Sit on the table!'). (Asher 1977: 31)

Learners are also required to produce novel combinations of their own.

Learners monitor and evaluate their own progress. They are encouraged to speak when they feel ready to speak – that is, when a sufficient basis in the language has been internalized.

Teacher roles

The teacher plays an active and direct role in Total Physical Response. "The instructor is the director of a stage play in which the students are the actors" (Asher 1977: 43). It is the teacher who decides what to teach, who models and presents the new materials, and who selects supporting materials for classroom use. The teacher is encouraged to be well prepared and well organized so that the lesson flows smoothly and predictably. Asher recommends detailed lesson plans: "It is wise to write out the exact utterances you will be using and especially the novel commands because the action is so fast-moving there is usually not time for you to create spontaneously" (1977: 47). Classroom interaction and turn taking is teacher rather than learner directed. Even when learners interact with other learners it is usually the teacher who initiates the interaction:

Teacher: Maria, pick up the box of rice and hand it to Miguel and ask Miguel to read the price.

Asher stresses, however, that the teacher's role is not so much to teach as to provide opportunities for learning. The teacher has the responsibility of providing the best kind of exposure to language so that the learner can internalize the basic rules of the target language. Thus the teacher controls the language input the learners receive, providing the raw material for the "cognitive map" that the learners will construct in their own minds. The teacher should also allow speaking abilities to develop in learners at the learners' own natural pace.

In giving feedback to learners, the teacher should follow the example of parents giving feedback to their children. At first, parents correct very little, but as the child grows older, parents are said to tolerate fewer mistakes in speech. Similarly teachers should refrain from too much correction in the early stages and should not interrupt to correct errors, since this will inhibit learners. As time goes on, however, more teacher intervention is expected, as the learners' speech becomes "fine tuned."

Asher cautions teachers about preconceptions that he feels could hinder the successful implementation of TPR principles. First, he cautions against the "illusion of simplicity," where the teacher underestimates the difficulties involved in learning a foreign language. This results in progressing at too fast a pace and failing to provide a gradual transition from one teaching stage to another. The teacher should also avoid having too narrow a tolerance for errors in speaking.

You begin with a wide tolerance for student speech errors, but as training progresses, the tolerance narrows. . . . Remember that as students progress in their training, more and more attention units are freed to process feedback from the instructor. In the beginning, almost no attention units are available to hear the instructor's attempts to correct distortions in speech. All attention is directed to producing utterances. Therefore the student cannot attend efficiently to the instructor's corrections. (Asher 1977: 27)

The role of instructional materials

There is generally no basic text in a Total Physical Response course. Materials and realia play an increasing role, however, in later learning stages. For absolute beginners, lessons may not require the use of materials, since the teacher's voice, actions, and gestures may be a sufficient basis for classroom activities. Later the teacher may use common classroom objects, such as books, pens, cups, furniture. As the course develops, the teacher will need to make or collect supporting materials to support teaching points. These may include pictures, realia, slides, and word charts. Asher has developed TPR student kits that focus on specific situations, such as the home, the supermarket, the beach. Students may use the kits to construct scenes (e.g., "Put the stove in the kitchen").

Procedure

Asher (1977) provides a lesson-by-lesson account of a course taught according to TPR principles, which serves as a source of information on the procedures used in the TPR classroom. The course was for adult immigrants and consisted of 159 hours of classroom instruction. The sixth class in the course proceeded in the following way:

Review. This was a fast-moving warm-up in which individual students were moved with commands such as:

Pablo, drive your car around Miako and honk your horn.
Jeffe, throw the red flower to Maria.
Maria, scream.
Rita, pick up the knife and spoon and put them in the cup.
Eduardo, take a drink of water and give the cup to Elaine.

New commands. These verbs were introduced.

wash	your hands.
	your face.
	your hair.
	the cup.
look for	a towel.
	the soap.
	a comb.
hold	the book.
	the cup.
	the soap.
comb	your hair.
	Maria's hair.
	Shirou's hair.
brush	your teeth.
	your pants.
	the table.

Other items introduced were:

Rectangle   Draw a rectangle on the chalkboard.
                Pick up a rectangle from the table and give it to me.
                Put the rectangle next to the square.

Triangle   Pick up the triangle from the table and give it to me.
                Catch the triangle and put it next to the rectangle.

Quickly   Walk quickly to the door and hit it.
                Quickly, run to the table and touch the square.
                Sit down quickly and laugh.

Slowly   Walk slowly to the window and jump.
                Slowly, stand up.
                Slowly walk to me and hit me on the arm.

Toothpaste   Look for the toothpaste.
                Throw the toothpaste to Wing.
                Wing, unscrew the top of the toothpaste.

Toothbrush   Take out your toothbrush.
                Brush your teeth.
                Put your toothbrush in your book.

Teeth   Touch your teeth.
                Show your teeth to Dolores.
                Dolores, point to Eduardo's teeth.

Soap   Look for the soap.
                Give the soap to Elaine.
                Elaine, put the soap in Ramiro's ear.

Towel   Put the towel on Juan's arm.
                Juan, put the towel on your head and laugh.
                Maria, wipe your hands on the towel.

Next, the instructor asked simple questions which the student could answer with a gesture such as pointing. Examples would be:

Where is the towel? [Eduardo, point to the towel!]
Where is the toothbrush? [Miako, point to the toothbrush!]
Where is Dolores?

Role reversal. Students readily volunteered to utter commands that manipulated the behavior of the instructor and other students....

Reading and writing. The instructor wrote on the chalkboard each new vocabulary item and a sentence to illustrate the item. Then she spoke each item and acted out the sentence. The students listened as she read the material. Some copied the information in their notebooks.

(Asher 1977: 54–6)

Conclusion

Total Physical Response is in a sense a revival and extension of Palmer and Palmer's *English Through Actions*, updated with references to more recent psychological theories. It has enjoyed some popularity because of its support by those who emphasize the role of comprehension in second language acquisition. Krashen (1981), for example, regards provision of comprehensible input and reduction of stress as keys to successful language acquisition, and he sees performing physical actions in the target language as a means of making input comprehensible and minimizing stress (see Chapter 9). The experimental support for the effectiveness of Total Physical Response is sketchy (as it is for most methods) and typically deals with only the very beginning stages of learning. Proponents of Communicative Language Teaching would question the relevance to real-world learner needs of the TPR syllabus and the utterances and sentences used within it. Asher himself, however, has stressed that Total Physical Response should be used in association with other methods and techniques. Indeed, practitioners of TPR typically follow this recommendation, suggesting that for many teachers TPR represents a useful set of techniques and is compatible with other approaches to teaching. TPR practices therefore may be effective for reasons other than those proposed by Asher and do not necessarily demand commitment to the learning theories used to justify them.

Bibliography

Asher, J. 1965. The strategy of the today physical response: an application to learning Russian. *International Review of Applied Linguistics* 3: 291–300.

Asher, J. 1966. The learning strategy of the total physical response: a review. *Modern Language Journal* 50: 79–84.

Asher, J. 1969. The total physical response approach to second language learning. *Modern Language Journal* 53: 3–17.

Asher, J. 1972. Children's first language as a model of second language learning. *Modern Language Journal* 56: 133–9.

Asher, J. 1977. *Learning Another Language Through Actions: The Complete Teacher's Guide Book*. Los Gatos, Calif.: Sky Oaks Productions. (2nd ed. 1982.)

Asher, J. 1981a. The extinction of second language learning in American schools: an intervention model. In H. Winitz (ed.), *The Comprehension Approach* to *Foreign Language Instruction*, pp. 49–68. Rowley, Mass.: Newbury House.

Asher, J. 1981b. The fear of foreign languages. *Psychology Today* 15(8): 52–9.

Asher, J., J. A. Kusudo, and R. De La Torre. 1974. Learning a second language through commands: the second field test. *Modern Language Journal* 58: 24–32.

Asher, J., and B. S. Price. 1967. The learning strategy of the total physical response: some age differences. *Child Development* 38: 1219–27.

DeCecco, J. P. 1968. *The Psychology of Learning and Instruction: Educational Psychology*. Englewood Cliffs, N.J.: Prentice-Hall.

Katona, G. 1940. *Organizing and Memorizing: Studies in the Psychology of Learning and Teaching*. New York: Columbia University Press.

Krashen, S. D. 1981. *Second Language Acquisition and Second Language Learning*. Oxford: Pergamon.

Kunihira, S., and J. Asher. 1965. The strategy of the total physical response: an application to learning Japanese. *International Review of Applied Linguistics* 3: 277–89.

Miller, G. A., E. Galanter, and K. H. Pribram. 1960. *Plans and the Structure of Behavior*. New York: Henry Holt.

Palmer, H., and D. Palmer. 1925. *English Through Actions*. Reprint ed. London: Longman Green, 1959.

Winitz, H. (ed.). 1981. *The Comprehension Approach to Foreign Language Instruction*. Rowley, Mass.: Newbury House.

Winitz, H., and J. Reeds. 1975. *Comprehension and Problem Solving as Strategies for Language Training*. The Hague: Mouton.

Yorio, C. 1980. Conventionalized language forms and the development of communicative competence. *TESOL Quarterly* 14(4): 433–42.

7 The Silent Way

Background

The Silent Way is the name of a method of language teaching devised by Caleb Gattegno. Gattegno's name is well known for his revival of interest in the use of colored wooden sticks called cuisenaire rods and for his series Words in Color, an approach to the teaching of initial reading in which sounds are coded by specific colors. His materials are copyrighted and marketed through an organization he operates called Educational Solutions Inc., in New York. The Silent Way represents Gattegno's venture into the field of foreign language teaching. It is based on the premise that the teacher should be silent as much as possible in the classroom and the learner should be encouraged to produce as much language as possible. Elements of the Silent Way, particularly the use of color charts and the colored cuisenaire rods, grew out of Gattegno's previous experience as an educational designer of reading and mathematics programs. (Cuisenaire rods were first developed by Georges Cuisenaire, a European educator who used them for the teaching of math. Gattegno had observed Cuisenaire and this gave him the idea for their use in language teaching.)

The Silent Way shares a great deal with other learning theories and educational philosophies. Very broadly put, the learning hypotheses underlying Gattegno's work could be stated as follows:

1. Learning is facilitated if the learner discovers or creates rather than remembers and repeats what is to be learned.
2. Learning is facilitated by accompanying (mediating) physical objects.
3. Learning is facilitated by problem solving involving the material to be learned.

Let us consider each of these issues in turn.

1. The educational psychologist and philosopher Jerome Bruner distinguishes two traditions of teaching – that which takes place in the expository mode and that which takes place in the hypothetical mode. In the expository mode "decisions covering the mode and pace and style of exposition are principally determined by the teacher as expositor; the student is the listener." In the hypothetical mode "the teacher and the student are in a more cooperative position. The student is not a bench-

bound listener, but is taking part in the formulation and at times may play the principal role in it" (Bruner 1966: 83).

The Silent Way belongs to the latter tradition, which views learning as a problem-solving, creative, discovering activity, in which the learner is a principal actor rather than a bench-bound listener. Bruner discusses the benefits derived from "discovery learning" under four headings: (a) the increase in intellectual potency, (b) the shift from extrinsic to intrinsic rewards, (c) the learning of heuristics by discovering, and (d) the aid to conserving memory (Bruner 1966: 83). As we shall see, Gattegno claims similar benefits from learners taught via the Silent Way.

2. The rods and the color-coded pronunciation charts (called Fidel charts) provide physical foci for student learning and also create memorable images to facilitate student recall. In psychological terms, these visual devices serve as associative mediators for student learning and recall. The psychological literature on mediation in learning and recall is voluminous but, for our purposes, can be briefly summarized in a quote from Earl Stevick:

If the use of associative mediators produces better retention than repetition does, it seems to be the case that the quality of the mediators and the student's personal investment in them may also have a powerful effect on memory. (Stevick 1976: 25)

3. The Silent Way is also related to a set of premises that we have called "problem-solving approaches to learning." These premises are succinctly represented in the words of Benjamin Franklin:

Tell me and I forget,
teach me and I remember,
involve me and I learn.

In the language of experimental psychology, the kind of subject involvement that promotes greatest learning and recall involves processing of material to be learned at the "greatest cognitive depth" (Craik 1973) or, for our purposes, involving the greatest amount of problem-solving activity. Memory research has demonstrated that the learner's "memory benefits from creatively searching out, discovering and depicting" (Bower and Winzenz 1970). In the Silent Way, "the teacher's strict avoidance of repetition forces alertness and concentration on the part of the learners" (Gattegno 1972: 80). Similarly, the learner's grappling with the problem of forming an appropriate and meaningful utterance in a new language leads the learner to realization of the language "through his own perceptual and analytical powers" (Selman 1977). The Silent Way student is expected to become "independent, autonomous and responsible" (Gattegno 1976) — in other words, a good problem solver in language.

Approach

Theory of language

Gattegno takes an openly skeptical view of the role of linguistic theory in language teaching methodology. He feels that linguistic studies "may be a specialization, [that] carry with them a narrow opening of one's sensitivity and perhaps serve very little towards the broad end in mind" (Gattegno 1972: 84). Gattegno views language itself "as a substitute for experience, so experience is what gives meaning to language" (Gattegno 1972: 8). We are not surprised then to see simulated experiences using tokens and picture charts as central elements in Silent Way teaching.

Considerable discussion is devoted to the importance of grasping the "spirit" of the language and not just its component forms. By the "spirit" of the language Gattegno is referring to the way each language is composed of phonological and suprasegmental elements that combine to give the language its unique sound system and melody. The learner must gain a "feel" for this aspect of the target language as soon as possible, though how the learner is to do this is not altogether clear.

By looking at the material chosen and the sequence in which it is presented in a Silent Way classroom, it is clear that the Silent Way takes a structural approach to the organization of language to be taught. Language is seen as groups of sounds arbitrarily associated with specific meanings and organized into sentences or strings of meaningful units by grammar rules. Language is separated from its social context and taught through artificial situations, usually represented by rods. Lessons follow a sequence based on grammatical complexity, and new lexical and structural material is meticulously broken down into its elements, with one element presented at a time. The sentence is the basic unit of teaching, and the teacher focuses on propositional meaning, rather than communicative value. Students are presented with the structural patterns of the target language and learn the grammar rules of the language through largely inductive processes.

Gattegno sees vocabulary as a central dimension of language learning and the choice of vocabulary as crucial. He distinguishes between several classes of vocabulary items. The "semi-luxury vocabulary" consists of expressions common in the daily life of the target language culture; this refers to food, clothing, travel, family life, and so on. "Luxury vocabulary" is used in communicating more specialized ideas, such as political or philosophical opinions. The most important vocabulary for the learner deals with the most functional and versatile words of the language, many of which may not have direct equivalents in the learner's native tongue. This "functional vocabulary" provides a key, says Gattegno, to comprehending the "spirit" of the language.

Theory of learning

Like many other method proponents, Gattegno makes extensive use of his understanding of first language learning processes as a basis for deriving principles for teaching foreign languages to adults. Gattegno recommends, for example, that the learner needs to "return to the state of mind that characterizes a baby's learning – surrender" (Scott and Page 1982: 273).

Having referred to these processes, however, Gattegno states that the processes of learning a second language are "radically different" from those involved in learning a first language. The second language learner is unlike the first language learner and "cannot learn another language in the same way because of what he now knows" (Gattegno 1972: 11). The "natural" or "direct" approaches to acquiring a second language are thus misguided, says Gattegno, and a successful second language approach will "replace a 'natural' approach by one that is very 'artificial' and, for some purposes, strictly controlled" (1972: 12).

The "artificial approach" that Gattegno proposes is based on the principle that successful learning involves commitment of the self to language acquisition through the use of silent awareness and then active trial. Gattegno's repeated emphasis on the primacy of learning over teaching places a focus on the self of the learner, on the learner's priorities and commitments.

To speak . . . requires the descent of the will into the voluntary speech organs and a clear grasp by one's linguistic self of what one is to do to produce definite sounds in definite ways. Only the self of the utterer can intervene to make objective what it holds in itself. Every student must be seen as a will capable of that work. (Gattegno 1976: 7)

The self, we are told, consists of two systems – a learning system and a retaining system. The learning system is activated only by way of intelligent awareness. "The learner must constantly test his powers to abstract, analyze, synthesize and integrate" (Scott and Page 1982: 273). Silence is considered the best vehicle for learning, because in silence students concentrate on the task to be accomplished and the potential means to its accomplishment. Repetition (as opposed to silence) "consumes time and encourages the scattered mind to remain scattered" (Gattegno 1976: 80). Silence, as avoidance of repetition, is thus an aid to alertness, concentration, and mental organization.

The "retaining system" allows us to remember and recall at will linguistic elements and their organizing principles and makes linguistic communication possible. Gattegno speaks of remembering as a matter of "paying ogdens." An "ogden" is a unit of mental energy required to link permanently two mental elements, such as a shape and a sound or a label and an object. The forging of the link through active attention is the cost of remembering paid in ogdens. Retention by way of mental effort, awareness, and thoughtfulness is more efficient in terms of ogdens consumed than is retention attained through mechanical repetition. Again, silence is a key to triggering awareness and hence the preferred path to retention. Retention links are in fact formed in the most silent of periods, that of sleep: "The mind does much of this work during sleep" (Stevick 1980: 41).

Awareness is educable. As one learns "in awareness," one's powers of awareness and one's capacity to learn become greater. The Silent Way thus claims to facilitate what psychologists call "learning to learn." Again, the process chain that develops awareness proceeds from attention, production, self-correction, and absorption. Silent Way learners acquire "inner criteria," which play a central role "in one's education throughout all of one's life" (Gattegno 1976: 29). These inner criteria allow learners to monitor and self-correct their own production. It is in the activity of self-correction through self-awareness that the Silent Way claims to differ most notably from other ways of language learning. It is this capacity for self-awareness that the Silent Way calls upon, a capacity said to be little appreciated or exercised by first language learners.

But the Silent Way is not merely a language teaching method. Gattegno sees language learning through the Silent Way as a recovery of innocence — "a return to our full powers and potentials." Gattegno's aim is not just second language learning; it is nothing less than the education of the spiritual powers and of the sensitivity of the individual. Mastery of linguistic skills are seen in the light of an emotional inner peace resulting from the sense of power and control brought about by new levels of awareness. Silent Way learning claims to "consolidate the human dimensions of being, which include variety and individuality as essential factors for an acceptance of others as contributors to one's own life" and even moves us "towards better and more lasting solutions of present-day conflicts" (Gattegno 1972: 84).

Design

Objectives

The general objective of the Silent Way is to give beginning level students oral and aural facility in basic elements of the target language. The general goal set for language learning is near-native fluency in the target language, and correct pronunciation and mastery of the prosodic elements of the target language are emphasized. An immediate objective is to provide the learner with a basic practical knowledge of the grammar of the language. This forms the basis for independent learning on the learner's part. Gattegno discusses the following kinds of objectives as appropriate for a language course at an elementary level (Gattegno 1972: 81–83). Students should be able to

correctly and easily answer questions about themselves, their education, their family, travel, and daily events;
speak with a good accent;
give either a written or oral description of a picture, "including the existing relationships that concern space, time and numbers";
answer general questions about the culture and the literature of the native speakers of the target language;
perform adequately in the following areas: spelling, grammar (production rather than explanation), reading comprehension, and writing.

Gattegno states that the Silent Way teaches learners *how* to learn a language, and the skills developed through the process of learning a foreign or second language can be employed in dealing with "unknowns" of every type. The method, we are told, can also be used to teach reading and writing, and its usefulness is not restricted to beginning level students. Most of the examples Gattegno describes, however, as well as the classes we have observed, deal primarily with a basic level of aural/ oral proficiency.

The syllabus

The Silent Way adopts a basically structural syllabus, with lessons planned around grammatical items and related vocabulary. Gattegno does not, however, provide details as to the precise selection and arrangement of grammatical and lexical items to be covered. There is no general Silent Way syllabus. But from observation of Silent Way programs developed by the Peace Corps to teach a variety of languages at a basic level of proficiency, it is clear that language items are introduced according to their grammatical complexity, their relationship to what has been taught previously, and the ease with which items can be presented visually. Typically, the imperative is the initial structure introduced, because of the ease with which action verbs may be demonstrated using Silent Way materials. New elements, such as the plural form of nouns, are taught within a structure already familiar. Numeration occurs early in a course, because of the importance of numbers in everyday life and the ease with which they can be demonstrated. Prepositions of location also appear early in the syllabus for similar reasons.

Vocabulary is selected according to the degree to which it can be manipulated within a given structure and according to its productivity within the classroom setting. In addition to prepositions and numbers, pronouns, quantifiers, words dealing with temporal relations, and words of comparison are introduced early in the course, because they "refer to oneself and to others in the numerous relations of everyday life" (Stevick 1979). These kinds of words are referred to as the "functional vocabulary" of a language because of their high utility.

The following is a section of a Peace Corps Silent Way Syllabus for the first ten hours of instruction in Thai. It is used to teach American Peace Corps volunteers being trained to teach in Thailand. At least 15 minutes of every hour of instruction would be spent on pronunciation. A word that is italicized can be substituted for by another word having the same function.

Lesson	*Vocabulary*
1. Wood color *red*.	wood, red, green, yellow, brown, pink, white, orange, black, color
2. Using the numbers 1–10	one, two, ... ten
3. Wood color *red* two pieces.	
4. Take (pick up) wood color *red* two pieces.	take (pick up)
5. Take wood color *red* two pieces give *him*.	give, object pronouns
6. Wood *red* where? Wood *red on* table.	where, on, under, near, far, over, next to, here, there
7. Wood color red on table, *is it?* Yes, on. Not on.	Question-forming rules. Yes. No.
8. Wood color *red long*. Wood color green *longer*. Wood color orange *longest*.	adjectives of comparison
9. Wood color *green taller*. Wood color *red* is it?	
10. Review. Students use structures taught in new situations, such as comparing the heights of students in the class.	

(Joel Wiskin, personal communication)

Types of learning and teaching activities

Learning tasks and activities in the Silent Way have the function of encouraging and shaping student oral response without direct oral instruction from or unnecessary modeling by the teacher. Basic to the method are simple linguistic tasks in which the teacher models a word, phrase, or sentence and then elicits learner responses. Learners then go on to create their own utterances by putting together old and new information. Charts, rods, and other aids may be used to elicit learner responses. Teacher modeling is minimal, although much of the activity may be teacher directed. Responses to commands, questions, and visual cues thus constitute the basis for classroom activities.

Learner roles

Gattegno sees language learning as a process of personal growth resulting from growing student awareness and self-challenge. The learner first experiences a "random or almost random feeling of the area of activity in question until one finds one or more cornerstones to build on. Then starts a systematic analysis, first by trial and error, later by directed experiment with practice of the acquired subareas until mastery follows" (Gattegno 1972: 79). Learners are expected to develop independence, autonomy, and responsibility. Independent learners are those who are aware that they must depend on their own resources and realize that they can use "the knowledge of their own language to open up some things in a new language" or that they can "take their knowledge of the first few words in the new language and figure out additional words by using that knowledge" (Stevick 1980: 42). The autonomous learner chooses proper expressions in a given set of circumstances and situations. "The teacher cultivates the student's 'autonomy' by deliberately building choices into situations" (Stevick 1980: 42). Responsible learners know that they have free will to choose among any set of linguistic choices. The ability to choose intelligently and carefully is said to be evidence of responsibility. The absence of correction and repeated modeling from the teacher requires the students to develop "inner criteria" and to correct themselves. The absence of explanations requires learners to make generalizations, come to their own conclusions, and formulate whatever rules they themselves feel they need.

Learners exert a strong influence over each other's learning and, to a lesser degree, over the linguistic content taught. They are expected to interact with each other and suggest alternatives to each other. Learners have only themselves as individuals and the group to rely on, and so must learn to work cooperatively rather than competitively. They need to feel comfortable both correcting each other and being corrected by each other.

In order to be productive members of the learning group, learners thus have to play varying roles. At times one is an independent individual, at other times a group member. A learner also must be a teacher, a student, part of a support system, a problem solver, and a self-evaluator. And it is the student who is usually expected to decide on what role is most appropriate to a given situation.

Teacher roles

Teacher silence is, perhaps, the unique and, for many traditionally trained language teachers, the most demanding aspect of the Silent Way. Teachers are exhorted to resist their long standing commitment to model, remodel, assist, and direct desired student responses, and Silent Way teachers have remarked upon the arduousness of self-restraint to which early experience of the Silent Way has subjected them. Gattegno talks of subordinating "teaching to learning," but that is not to suggest that the teacher's role in Silent Way is not critical and demanding. Gattegno anticipates that using the Silent Way would require most teachers to change their perception of their role. Stevick defines the Silent Way teacher's tasks as (a) to teach, (b) to test, and (c) to get out of the way (Stevick 1980: 56). Although this may not seem to constitute a radical alternative to standard teaching practice, the details of the steps the teacher is expected to follow are unique to the Silent Way.

By "teaching" is meant the presentation of an item once, typically using nonverbal clues to get across meanings. Testing follows immediately and might better be termed elicitation and shaping of student production, which, again, is done in as silent a way as possible. Finally, the teacher silently monitors learners' interactions with each other and may even leave the room while learners struggle with their new linguistic tools and "pay their ogdens." For the most part, Silent Way teacher's manuals are unavailable (however, see Arnold 1981), and teachers are responsible for designing teaching sequences and creating individual lessons and lesson elements. Gattegno emphasizes the importance of teacher-defined learning goals that are clear and attainable. Sequence and timing in Silent Way classes are more important than in many kinds of language teaching classes, and the teachers' sensitivity to and management of them is critical.

More generally, the teacher is responsible for creating an environment that encourages student risk taking and that facilitates learning. This is not to say that the Silent Way teacher becomes "one of the group." In fact, observers have noted that Silent Way teachers often appear aloof or even gruff with their students. The teacher's role is one of neutral observer, neither elated by correct performance nor discouraged by error. Students are expected to come to see the teacher as a disinterested judge, supportive but emotionally uninvolved.

The teacher uses gestures, charts, and manipulatives in order to elicit and shape student responses and so must be both facile and creative as a pantomimist and puppeteer. In sum, the Silent Way teacher, like the complete dramatist, writes the script, chooses the props, sets the mood, models the action, designates the players, and is critic for the performance.

The role of instructional materials

The Silent Way is perhaps as well known for the unique nature of its teaching materials as for the silence of its teachers. The materials consist mainly of a set of colored rods, color-coded pronunciation and vocabulary wall charts, a pointer, and reading/writing exercises, all of which are used to illustrate the relationships between sound and meaning in the target language. The materials are designed for manipulation by the students as well as by the teacher, independently and cooperatively, in promoting language learning by direct association.

The pronunciation charts, called "Fidels," have been devised for a number of languages and contain symbols in the target language for all of the vowel and consonant sounds of the language. The symbols are color coded according to pronunciation; thus, if a language possesses two different symbols for the same sound, they will be colored alike. Classes often begin by using Fidel charts in the native language, color coded in an analogous manner, so that students learn to pair a sound with its associated color. There may be from one to eight of such charts, depending upon the language. The teacher uses the pointer to indicate a sound symbol for the students to produce. Where native-language Fidels are used, the teacher will point to a symbol on one chart and then to its analogue on the Fidel in the other language. In the absence of native-language charts, or when introducing a sound not present in the native language, the teacher will give one clear, audible model after indicating the proper Fidel symbol in the target language. The charts are hung on the wall and serve to aid in remembering pronunciation and in building new words by sounding out sequences of symbols as they are pointed to by the teacher or student.

Just as the Fidel charts are used to visually illustrate pronunciation, the colored cuisenaire rods are used to directly link words and structures with their meanings in the target language, thereby avoiding translation into the native language. The rods vary in length from one to ten centimeters, and each length has a specific color. The rods may be used for naming colors, for size comparisons, to represent people, build floor plans, constitute a road map, and so on. Use of the rods is intended to promote inventiveness, creativity, and interest in forming communicative utterances on the part of the students, as they move from simple to more complex structures. Gattegno and his proponents believe that the range of structures that can be illustrated and learned through skillful use of the rods is as limitless as the human imagination. When the teacher or student has difficulty expressing a desired word or concept, the rods can be supplemented by referring to the Fidel charts, or to the third major visual aid used in the Silent Way, the vocabulary charts.

The vocabulary or word charts are likewise color coded, although the colors of the symbols will not correspond to the phonetics of the Fidels, but rather to conceptual groupings of words. There are typically twelve such charts containing 500 to 800 words in the native language and script. These words are selected according to their ease of application in teaching, their relative place in the "functional" or "luxury" vocabulary, their flexibility in terms of generalization and use with other words, and their importance in illustrating basic grammatical structures. The content of word charts will vary from language to language, but the general content of the vocabulary charts (Gattegno 1972) is paraphrased below:

Chart 1:	the word *rod*, colors of the rods, plural markers, simple imperative verbs, personal pronouns, some adjectives and question words
Charts 2, 3:	remaining pronouns, words for "here" and "there," *of, for,* and *name*
Chart 4:	numbers
Charts 5, 6:	words illustrating size, space, and temporal relationships, as well as some concepts difficult to illustrate with rods, such as order, causality, condition, similarity and difference
Chart 7:	words that qualify, such as adverbs
Charts 8, 9:	verbs, with cultural references where possible
Chart 10:	family relationships
Charts 11, 12:	words expressing time, calendar elements, seasons, days, *week, month, year,* etc.

Other materials that may be used include books and worksheets for practicing reading and writing skills, picture books, tapes, videotapes, films, and other visual aids. Reading and writing are sometimes taught from the beginning, and students are given assignments to do outside the classroom at their own pace. These materials are of secondary importance, and are used to supplement the classroom use of rods and charts. Choice and implementation depends upon need as assessed by teachers and/or students.

Procedure

A Silent Way lesson typically follows a standard format. The first part of the lesson focuses on pronunciation. Depending on student level, the class might work on sounds, phrases, or even sentences designated on the Fidel chart. At the beginning stage, the teacher will model the appropriate sound after pointing to a symbol on the chart. Later, the teacher will silently point to individual symbols and combinations of symbols, and monitor student utterances. The teacher may say a word and have a student guess what sequence of symbols comprised the word.

109

The pointer is used to indicate stress, phrasing, and intonation. Stress can be shown by touching certain symbols more forcibly than others when pointing out a word. Intonation and phrasing can be demonstrated by tapping on the chart to the rhythm of the utterance.

After practice with the sounds of the language, sentence patterns, structure, and vocabulary are practiced. The teacher models an utterance while creating a visual realization of it with the colored rods. After modeling the utterance, the teacher will have a student attempt to produce the utterance and will indicate its acceptability. If a response is incorrect, the teacher will attempt to reshape the utterance or have another student present the correct model. After a structure is introduced and understood, the teacher will create a situation in which the students can practice the structure through the manipulation of the rods. Variations on the structural theme will be elicited from the class using the rods and charts.

The sample lesson that follows illustrates a typical lesson format. The language being taught is Thai, for which this is the first lesson.

1. Teacher empties rods onto the table.
2. Teacher picks up two or three rods of different colors, and after each rod is picked up says: [mai].
3. Teacher holds up one rod of any color and indicates to a student that a response is required. Student says: [mai]. If response is incorrect, teacher elicits response from another student, who then models for the first student.
4. Teacher next picks up a red rod and says: [mai sii daeng].
5. Teacher picks up a green rod and says: [mai sii khiaw].
6. Teacher picks up either a red or green rod and elicits response from student. If response is incorrect, procedure in step 3 is followed (student modeling).
7. Teacher introduces two or three other colors in the same manner.
8. Teacher shows any of the rods whose forms were taught previously and elicits student response. Correction technique is through student modeling, or the teacher may help student isolate error and self-correct.
9. When mastery is achieved, teacher puts one red rod in plain view and says: [mai sii daeng nung an].
10. Teacher then puts two red rods in plain view and says: [mai sii daeng song an].
11. Teacher places two green rods in view and says: [mai sii khiaw song an].
12. Teacher holds up two rods of a different color and elicits student response.
13. Teacher introduces additional numbers, based on what the class can comfortably retain. Other colors might also be introduced.
14. Rods are put in a pile. Teacher indicates, through his or her own actions, that rods should be picked up, and the correct utterance made. All the students in the group pick up rods and make utterances. Peer-group correction is encouraged.

15. Teacher then says: [kep mai sii daeng song an].
16. Teacher indicates that a student should give the teacher the rods called for. Teacher asks other students in the class to give him or her the rods that he or she asks for. This is all done in the target language through unambiguous actions on the part of the teacher.
17. Teacher now indicates that the students should give each other commands regarding the calling for of rods. Rods are put at the disposal of the class.
18. Experimentation is encouraged. Teacher speaks only to correct an incorrect utterance, if no peer group correction is forthcoming.

(Joel Wiskin, personal communication)

Conclusion

Despite the philosophical and sometimes almost metaphysical quality of much of Gattegno's writings, the actual practices of the Silent Way are much less revolutionary than might be expected. Working from what is a rather traditional structural and lexical syllabus, the method exemplifies many of the features that characterize more traditional methods, such as Situational Language Teaching and Audiolingualism, with a strong focus on accurate repetition of sentences modeled initially by the teacher and a movement through guided elicitation exercises to freer communication. The innovations in Gattegno's method derive primarily from the manner in which classroom activities are organized, the indirect role the teacher is required to assume in directing and monitoring learner performance, the responsibility placed upon learners to figure out and test their hypotheses about how the language works, and the materials used to elicit and practice language.

Bibliography

Arnold, F. 1981. *College English: A Silent-Way Approach*. Nara, Japan: Dawn Press.

Blair, R. W. (ed.). 1982. *Innovative Approaches to Language Teaching*. Rowley, Mass.: Newbury House.

Bower, G. H., and D. Winzenz. 1970. Comparison of associative learning strategies. *Psychonomic Sciences* 20: 119–20.

Bruner, J. 1966. *On Knowing: Essays for the Left Hand*. New York: Atheneum.

Craik, F. I. M. 1973. A levels of analysis view of memory. In P. Pliner, L. Krames, and T. Alloway (eds.), *Communication and Affect: Language and Thought*. New York: Academic Press.

Diller, K. C. 1978. *The Language Teaching Controversy*. Rowley, Mass.: Newbury House.

Gattegno, C. 1972. *Teaching Foreign Languages in Schools: The Silent Way.* 2nd ed. New York: Educational Solutions.

Gattegno, C. 1976. *The Common Sense of Teaching Foreign Languages.* New York: Educational Solutions.

Rossner, R. 1982. Talking shop: a conversation with Caleb Gattegno, inventor of the Silent Way. *ELT Journal* 36(4): 237–41.

Scott, R., and M. Page. 1982. The subordination of teaching to learning: a seminar conducted by Dr. Caleb Gattegno. *ELT Journal* 36(4): 273–4.

Selman, M. 1977. The silent way: insights for ESL. *TESL Talk* (8): 33–6.

Stevick, E. W. 1976. *Memory, Meaning and Method: Some Psychological Perspectives on Language Learning.* Rowley, Mass.: Newbury House.

Stevick, E. W. 1980. *Teaching Languages: A Way and Ways.* Rowley, Mass.: Newbury House.

Thompson, G. J. 1980. *The Silent Way: Interpretation and Application.* Master's thesis, University of Hawaii.

Varvel, T. 1979. The silent way: panacea or pipedream? *TESOL Quarterly* 13 (4): 483–94.

8 Community Language Learning

Background

Community Language Learning (CLL) is the name of a method developed by Charles A. Curran and his associates. Curran was a specialist in counseling and a professor of psychology at Loyola University, Chicago. His application of psychological counseling techniques to learning is known as Counseling-Learning. Community Language Learning represents the use of Counseling-Learning theory to teach languages.

Within the language teaching tradition Community Language Learning is sometimes cited as an example of a "humanistic approach." Links can also be made between CLL procedures and those of bilingual education, particularly the set of bilingual procedures referred to as "language alternation" or "code switching." Let us discuss briefly the debt of Community Language Learning to these traditions.

As the name indicates, CLL derives its primary insights, and indeed its organizing rationale, from Rogerian counseling. Counseling, as Rogerians see it, consists of one individual (the counselor) assuming "insofar as he is able the internal frame of reference [of the client], perceiving the world as that person sees it and communicating something of this empathetic understanding" (Rogers 1951). In lay terms, counseling is one person giving advice, assistance, and support to another who has a problem or is in some way in need. Community Language Learning draws on the counseling metaphor to redefine the roles of the teacher (the *counselor*) and learners (the *clients*) in the language classroom. The basic procedures of CLL can thus be seen as derived from the counselor–client relationship. Consider the following CLL procedures: A group of learners sit in a circle with the teacher standing outside the circle; a student whispers a message in the native language (L1); the teacher translates it into the foreign language (L2); the student repeats the message in the foreign language into a cassette; students compose further messages in the foreign language with the teacher's help; students reflect about their feelings. We can compare the client–counselor relationship in psychological counseling with the learner–knower relationship in Community Language Learning (Table 8.1).

CLL techniques also belong to a larger set of foreign language teaching

TABLE 8.1 COMPARISON OF CLIENT—COUNSELOR RELATIONSHIPS IN PSYCHO-
LOGICAL COUNSELING AND CLL

Psychological counseling (client–counselor)	*Community Language Learning (learner–knower)*
1. Client and counselor agree [contract] to counseling.	1. Learner and knower agree to language learning.
2. Client articulates his or her problem in language of affect.	2. Learner presents to the knower (in L1) a message he or she wishes to deliver to another.
3. Counselor listens carefully.	3. Knower listens and other learners overhear.
4. Counselor restates client message in language of cognition.	4. Knower restates learner's message in L2.
5. Client evaluates the accuracy of counselor's message restatement.	5. Learner repeats the L2 message form to its addressee.
6. Client reflects on the interaction of the counseling session.	6. Learner replays (from tape or memory) and reflects upon the messages exchanged during the language class.

practices sometimes described as *humanistic techniques* (Moskowitz 1978). Moskowitz defines humanistic techniques as those that

blend what the student feels, thinks and knows with what he is learning in the target language. Rather than self-denial being the acceptable way of life, self-actualization and self-esteem are the ideals the exercises pursue. [The techniques] help build rapport, cohesiveness, and caring that far transcend what is already there...help students to be themselves, to accept themselves, and be proud of themselves...help foster a climate of caring and sharing in the foreign language class. (Moskowitz 1978: 2)

In sum, humanistic techniques engage the whole person, including the emotions and feelings (the affective realm) as well as linguistic knowledge and behavioral skills.

Another language teaching tradition with which Community Language Learning is linked is a set of practices used in certain kinds of bilingual education programs and referred to by Mackey (1972) as "language alternation." In language alternation, a message/lesson/class is presented first in the native tongue and then again in the second language. Students know the meaning and flow of an L2 message from their recall of the parallel meaning and flow of an L1 message. They begin to holistically piece together a view of the language out of these message sets. In CLL, a learner presents a message in L1 to the knower. The message is translated into L2 by the knower. The learner then repeats the message in L2, addressing it to another learner with whom he or she wishes to communicate. CLL learners are encouraged to attend to the "overhears" they experience between other learners and their knowers. The result of the "overhear" is that every member of the group can understand what any given learner is trying to communicate (La Forge 1983: 45). In view of the reported success of language alternation procedures in several well-studied bilingual education settings (e.g., Lim 1968; Mackey 1972), it may be that this little-discussed aspect of CLL accounts for more of the informally reported successes of CLL students than is usually acknowledged.

Approach

Theory of language

Curran himself wrote little about his theory of language. His student La Forge (1983) has attempted to be more explicit about this dimension of Community Language Learning theory, and we draw on his account for the language theory underlying the method. La Forge reviews linguistic theory as a prelude to presenting the CLL model of language. He seems to accept that language theory must start, though not end, with criteria for sound features, the sentence, and abstract models of language (La Forge 1983: 4). The foreign language learners' tasks are "to apprehend the sound system, assign fundamental meanings, and to construct a basic grammar of the foreign language." He cites with pride that "after several months a small group of students was able to learn the basic sound and grammatical patterns of German" (1983: 47).

A theory of language built on "basic sound and grammatical patterns" does not appear to suggest any departures from traditional structuralist positions on the nature of language. However, the recent writings of CLL proponents deal at great length with what they call an alternative theory of language, which is referred to as *Language as Social Process*.

La Forge (1983) begins by suggesting that language as social process is "different from language as communication." We are led to infer that the concept of communication that La Forge rejects is the classic sender-message-receiver model in information theory. The social-process model is different from earlier information-transmitting models, La Forge suggests, because

communication is more than just a message being transmitted from a speaker to a listener. The speaker is at the same time both subject and object of his own message . . . communication involves not just the unidirectional transfer

115

of information to the other, but the very constitution of the speaking subject in relation to its other.... Communication is an exchange which is incomplete without a feedback reaction from the destinee of the message. (La Forge 1983: 3)

The information-transmission model and the social-process model of communication are compared in Figure 8.1.

The social-process view of language is then elaborated in terms of six qualities or subprocesses:

1. The whole-person process
2. The educational process
3. The interpersonal process
4. The developmental process
5. The communicative process
6. The cultural process

Explanation of these is beyond the scope of this chapter and, indeed, appears to involve elements outside a theory of language.

La Forge also elaborates on the interactional view of language underlying Community Language Learning (see Chapter 2). "Language is people; language is persons in contact; language is persons in response" (1983: 9). CLL interactions are of two distinct and fundamental kinds: interactions between learners and interactions between learners and knowers. Interactions between learners are unpredictable in content but typically are said to involve exchanges of affect. Learner exchanges deepen in intimacy as the class becomes a community of learners. The desire to be part of this growing intimacy pushes learners to keep pace with the learning of their peers. Tranel (1968) notes that "the students of the experimental group were highly motivated to learn in order to avoid isolation from the group." *Intimacy* then appears to be defined here as the desire to avoid isolation.

Interaction between learners and knowers is initially dependent. The learner tells the knower what he or she wishes to say in the target language, and the knower tells the learner how to say it. In later stages interactions between learner and knower are characterized as self-assertive (stage 2), resentful and indignant (stage 3), tolerant (stage 4), and independent (stage 5). These changes of interactive relationship are paralleled by five stages of language learning and five stages of affective conflicts (La Forge 1983: 50).

These two types of interactions may be said to be microcosmically equivalent to the two major classes of human interaction – interaction between equals (symmetrical) and interaction between unequals (asymmetrical) (Munby 1978). They also appear to represent examples of (a) interaction that changes in degree (learner to learner) and (b) interaction that changes in kind (learner to knower). That is, learner–learner inter-

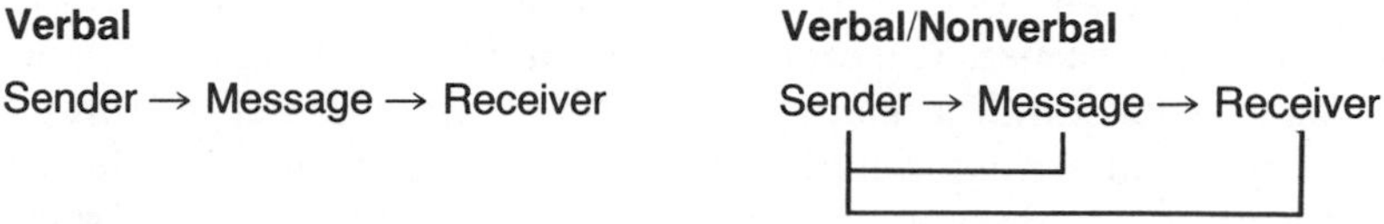

Verbal

Sender → Message → Receiver

Verbal/Nonverbal

Sender → Message → Receiver

Figure 8.1 Comparison of the information-transmission model (*left*) and the social-process model (*right*) of communication

action is held to change in the direction of increasing intimacy and trust, whereas learner–knower interaction is held to change in its very nature from dependent to resentful to tolerant to independent.

Theory of learning

Curran's counseling experience led him to conclude that the techniques of counseling could be applied to learning in general (this became Counseling-Learning) and to language teaching in particular (Community Language Learning). The CLL view of learning is contrasted with two other types of learning, which Curran saw as widespread and undesirable. The first of these describes a putative learning view long popular in Western culture. In this view, "the intellectual and factual process alone are regarded as the main intent of learning, to the neglect of engagement and involvement of the self" (Curran 1972: 58). The second view of learning is the behavioral view. Curran refers to this kind of learning as "animal learning," in which learners are "passive" and their involvement limited (Curran 1976: 84).

In contrast, CLL advocates a holistic approach to language learning, since "true" human learning is both cognitive and affective. This is termed *whole-person learning*. Such learning takes place in a communicative situation where teachers and learners are involved in "an interaction . . . in which both experience a sense of their own wholeness" (Curran 1972: 90). Within this, the development of the learner's relationship with the teacher is central. The process is divided into five stages and compared to the ontogenetic development of the child.

In the first, "birth" stage, feelings of security and belonging are established. In the second, as the learner's abilities improve, the learner, as child, begins to achieve a measure of independence from the parent. By the third, the learner "speaks independently" and may need to assert his or her own identity, often rejecting unasked-for advice. The fourth stage sees the learner as secure enough to take criticism, and by the last stage, the learner merely works upon improving style and knowledge of linguistic appropriateness. By the end of the process, the child has become adult. The learner knows everything the teacher does and can become knower for a new learner. The process of learning a new language, then, is like being reborn and developing a new persona, with all the trials and challenges that are associated with birth and maturation. Insofar as language learning is thought to develop through creating social relationships, success in language learning follows from a successful relationship between learner and teacher, and learner and learner. "Learning is viewed as a unified, personal and social experience." The learner "is no longer seen as learning in isolation and in competition with others" (Curran 1972: 11–12).

Curran in many places discusses what he calls "consensual validation," or "convalidation," in which mutual warmth, understanding, and a positive evaluation of the other person's worth develops between the teacher and the learner. A relationship characterized by convalidation is considered essential to the learning process and is a key element of CLL classroom procedures. A group of ideas concerning the psychological requirements for successful learning are collected under the acronym SARD (Curran 1976: 6), which can be explained as follows.

S stands for security. Unless learners feel secure, they will find it difficult to enter into a successful learning experience.

A stands for attention and aggression. CLL recognizes that a loss of attention should be taken as an indication of the learner's lack of involvement in learning, the implication being that variety in the choice of learner tasks will increase attention and therefore promote learning. Aggression applies to the way in which a child, having learned something, seeks an opportunity to show his or her strength by taking over and demonstrating what has been learned, using the new knowledge as a tool for self-assertion.

R stands for retention and reflection. If the whole person is involved in the learning process, what is retained is internalized and becomes a part of the learner's new persona in the foreign language. Reflection is a consciously identified period of silence within the framework of the lesson for the student "to focus on the learning forces of the last hour, to assess his present stage of development, and to re-evaluate future goals" (La Forge 1983: 68).

D denotes discrimination. When learners "have retained a body of material, they are ready to sort it out and see how one thing relates to another" (La Forge 1983: 69). This discrimination process becomes more refined and ultimately "enables the students to use the language for purposes of communication outside the classroom" (La Forge 1983: 69).

These central aspects of Curran's learning philosophy address not the psycholinguistic and cognitive processes involved in second language acquisition, but rather the personal commitments that learners need to

118

make before language acquisition processes can operate. CLL learning theory hence stands in marked contrast to linguistically or psycholinguistically based learned theories, such as those informing Audiolingualism or the Natural Approach.

Design

Objectives

Since linguistic or communicative competence is specified only in social terms, explicit linguistic or communicative objectives are not defined in the literature on Community Language Learning. Most of what has been written about CLL describes its use in introductory conversation courses in a foreign language. The assumption seems to be that through the method, the teacher can successfully transfer his or her knowledge and proficiency in the target language to the learners, which implies that attaining near-native like mastery of the target language is set as a goal. Specific objectives are not addressed.

The syllabus

Community Language Learning is most often used in the teaching of oral proficiency, but with some modifications it may be used in the teaching of writing, as Tranel (1968) has demonstrated. CLL does not use a conventional language syllabus, which sets out in advance the grammar, vocabulary, and other language items to be taught and the order in which they will be covered. If a course is based on Curran's recommended procedures, the course progression is topic based, with learners nominating things they wish to talk about and messages they wish to communicate to other learners. The teacher's responsibility is to provide a conveyance for these meanings in a way appropriate to the learners' proficiency level. Although CLL is not explicit about this, skilled CLL teachers seem to sift the learners' intentions through the teacher's implicit syllabus, providing translations that match what learners can be expected to do and say at that level. In this sense then a CLL syllabus emerges from the interaction between the learner's expressed communicative intentions and the teacher's reformulations of these into suitable target language utterances. Specific grammatical points, lexical patterns, and generalizations will sometimes be isolated by the teacher for more detailed study and analysis, and subsequent specification of these as a retrospective account of what the course covered could be a way of deriving a CLL language syllabus. Each CLL course would evolve its own syllabus, however, since what develops out of teacher–learner interactions in one course will be different from what happens in another.

Types of learning and teaching activities

As with most methods, CLL combines innovative learning tasks and activities with conventional ones. They include:

1. *Translation.* Learners form a small circle. A learner whispers a message or meaning he or she wants to express, the teacher translates it into (and may interpret it in) the target language, and the learner repeats the teacher's translation.
2. *Group Work.* Learners may engage in various group tasks, such as small-group discussion of a topic, preparing a conversation, preparing a summary of a topic for presentation to another group, preparing a story that will be presented to the teacher and the rest of the class.
3. *Recording.* Students record conversations in the target language.
4. *Transcription.* Students transcribe utterances and conversations they have recorded for practice and analysis of linguistic forms.
5. *Analysis.* Students analyze and study transcriptions of target language sentences in order to focus on particular lexical usage or on the application of particular grammar rules.
6. *Reflection and observation.* Learners reflect and report on their experience of the class, as a class or in groups. This usually consists of expressions of feelings – sense of one another, reactions to silence, concern for something to say, etc.
7. *Listening.* Students listen to a monologue by the teacher involving elements they might have elicited or overheard in class interactions.
8. *Free conversation.* Students engage in free conversation with the teacher or with other learners. This might include discussion of what they learned as well as feelings they had about how they learned.

Learner roles

In Community Language Learning, learners become members of a community – their fellow learners and the teacher – and learn through interacting with members of the community. Learning is not viewed as an individual accomplishment but as something that is achieved collaboratively. Learners are expected to listen attentively to the knower, to freely provide meanings they wish to express, to repeat target utterances without hesitation, to support fellow members of the community, to report deep inner feelings and frustrations as well as joy and pleasure, and to become counselors to other learners. CLL learners are typically grouped in a circle of six to twelve learners, with the number of knowers varying from one per group to one per student. CLL has also been used in larger school classes where special grouping arrangements are necessary, such as organizing learners in temporary pairs in facing parallel lines.

Learner roles are keyed to the five stages of language learning outlined earlier. The view of the learner is an organic one, with each new role growing developmentally out of the one preceding. These role changes are not easily or automatically achieved. They are in fact seen as outcomes of affective crises.

When faced with a new cognitive task, the learner must solve an affective crisis. With the solution of the five affective crises, one for each CLL stage, the student progresses from a lower to a higher stage of development. (La Forge 1983: 44)

Learning is a "whole person" process, and the learner at each stage is involved not just in the accomplishment of cognitive (language learning) tasks but in the solution of affective conflicts and "the respect for the enactment of values" as well (La Forge 1983: 55).

CLL compares language learning to the stages of human growth. In stage 1 the learner is like an infant, completely dependent on the knower for linguistic content. "A new self of the learner is generated or born in the target language" (La Forge 1983:45). The learner repeats utterances made by the teacher in the target language and "overhears" the interchanges between other learners and knowers.

In stage 2 the "child achieves a measure of independence from the parent" (La Forge 1983: 46). Learners begin to establish their own self-affirmation and independence by using simple expressions and phrases they have previously heard.

In stage 3, "the separate-existence stage," learners begin to understand others directly in the target language. Learners will resent uninvited assistance provided by the knower/parent at this stage.

Stage 4 may be considered "a kind of adolescence." The learner functions independently, although his or her knowledge of the foreign language is still rudimentary. The role of "psychological understanding" shifts from knower to learner. The learner must learn how to elicit from the knower the advanced level of linguistic knowledge the knower possesses.

Stage 5 is called "the independent stage." Learners refine their understanding of register as well as grammatically correct language use. They may become counselors to less advanced students while profiting from contact with their original knower.

Teacher roles

At the deepest level, the teacher's function derives from the functions of the counselor in Rogerian psychological counseling. A counselor's

121

clients are people with problems, who in a typical counseling session will often use emotional language to communicate their difficulties to the counselor. The counselor's role is to respond calmly and nonjudgmentally, in a supportive manner, and help the client try to understand his or her problems better by applying order and analysis to them. The counselor is *not* responsible for paraphrasing the client's problem element for element but rather for capturing the essence of the client's concern, such that the client might say, "Yes, that's exactly what I meant." "One of the functions of the counseling response is to relate affect . . . to cognition. Understanding the language of 'feeling', the counselor replies in the language of cognition" (Curran 1976: 26). It was the model of teacher as counselor that Curran attempted to bring to language learning.

There is also room for actual counseling in Community Language Learning. Explicit recognition is given to the psychological problems that may arise in learning a second language. "Personal learning conflicts . . . anger, anxiety and similar psychological disturbance – understood and responded to by the teacher's counseling sensitivity – are indicators of deep personal investment" (J. Rardin, in Curran 1976: 103). In this case, the teacher is expected to play a role very close to that of the "regular" counselor. The teacher's response may be of a different order of detachment, consideration, and understanding from that of the average teacher in the same circumstances.

More specific teacher roles are, like those of the students, keyed to the five developmental stages. In the early stages of learning the teacher operates in a supportive role, providing target language translations and a model for imitation on request of the clients. Later, interaction may be initiated by the students, and the teacher monitors learner utterances, providing assistance when requested. As learning progresses, students become increasingly capable of accepting criticism, and the teacher may intervene directly to correct deviant utterances, supply idioms, and advise on usage and fine points of grammar. The teacher's role is initially likened to that of a nurturing parent. The student gradually "grows" in ability, and the nature of the relationship changes so that the teacher's position becomes somewhat dependent upon the learner. The knower derives a sense of self-worth through requests for the knower's assistance.

One continuing role of the teacher is particularly notable in Community Language Learning. The teacher is responsible for providing a safe environment in which clients can learn and grow. Learners, feeling secure, are free to direct their energies to the tasks of communication and learning rather than to building and maintaining their defensive positions. Curran describes the importance of a secure atmosphere as follows:

As whole persons, we seem to learn best in an atmosphere of personal security. Feeling secure, we are freed to approach the learning situation with the attitude of willing openness. Both the learner's and the knower's level of security determine the psychological tone of the entire learning experience. (Curran 1976: 6)

Many of the newer nontraditional language teaching methods we discuss in this book stress teacher responsibility for creating and maintaining a secure environment for learning; probably no method attaches greater importance to this aspect of language learning than does Community Language Learning. Thus, it is interesting to note two "asides" in the discussion of learning security in CLL.

First, security is a culturally relative concept. What provides a sense of security in one cultural context may produce anxiety in another. La Forge gives as an example the different patterns of personal introduction and how these are differentially expressed and experienced in early stages of CLL among students of different backgrounds. "Each culture had unique forms which provide for acquaintance upon forming new groups. These must be carefully adopted so as to provide cultural security for the students of the foreign language" (La Forge 1983: 66).

Second, it may be undesirable to create too secure an environment for learners. "The security of the students is never absolute: otherwise no learning would occur" (La Forge 1983: 65). This is reminiscent of the teacher who says, "My students would never learn anything if the fear of examination failure didn't drive them to it." How much insecurity is optimal for language learning in Community Language Learning is unfortunately not further discussed in the literature.

The role of instructional materials

Since a CLL course evolves out of the interactions of the community, a textbook is not considered a necessary component. A textbook would impose a particular body of language content on the learners, thereby impeding their growth and interaction. Materials may be developed by the teacher as the course develops, although these generally consist of little more than summaries on the blackboard or overhead projector of some of the linguistic features of conversations generated by students. Conversations may also be transcribed and distributed for study and analysis, and learners may work in groups to produce their own materials, such as scripts for dialogues and mini-dramas.

In early accounts of CLL the use of teaching machines (the Chromachord Teaching System) is recommended for necessary "rote-drill and practice" in language learning. "The ... design and use of machines ... now appear[s] to make possible the freeing of the teacher to do what only a *human person* can do ... become a learning counselor" (Curran 976: 6). In more recent CLL descriptions (e.g., La Forge 1983) teaching machines and their accompanying materials are not mentioned, and we assume that contemporary CLL classes do not use teaching machines at all.

Procedure

Since each Community Language Learning course is in a sense a unique experience, description of typical CLL procedures in a class period is problematic. Stevick distinguishes between "classical" CLL (based directly on the model proposed by Curran) and personal interpretations of it, such as those discussed by different advocates of CLL (e.g., La Forge 1983). The following description attempts to capture some typical activities in CLL classes.

Generally the observer will see a circle of learners all facing one another. The learners are linked in some way to knowers or a single knower as teacher. The first class (and subsequent classes) may begin with a period of silence, in which learners try to determine what is supposed to happen in their language class. In later classes, learners may sit in silence while they decide what to talk about (La Forge 1983: 72). The observer may note that the awkwardness of silence becomes sufficiently agonizing for someone to volunteer to break the silence. The knower may use the volunteered comment as a way of introducing discussion of classroom contacts or as a stimulus for language interaction regarding how learners felt about the period of silence. The knower may encourage learners to address questions to one another or to the knower. These may be questions on any subject a learner is curious enough to inquire about. The questions and answers may be tape recorded for later use, as reminder and review of topics discussed and language used.

The teacher might then form the class into facing lines for three-minute pair conversations. These are seen as equivalent to the brief wrestling sessions by which judo students practice. Following this the class might be reformed into small groups in which a single topic, chosen by the class or the group, is discussed. The summary of the group discussion may be presented to another group, who in turn try to repeat or paraphrase the summary back to the original group.

In an intermediate or advanced class a teacher may encourage groups to prepare a paper drama for presentation to the rest of the class. A paper drama group prepares a story that is told or shown to the counselor. The counselor provides or corrects target language statements and suggests improvements to the story sequence. Students are then given materials with which they prepare large picture cards to accompany their story. After practicing the story dialogue and preparing the accompanying pictures, each group presents its paper drama to the rest of the class. The students accompany their story with music, puppets, and drums as well as with their pictures (La Forge 1983: 81–2).

Finally, the teacher asks learners to reflect on the language class, as a class or in groups. Reflection provides the basis for discussion of contracts (written or oral contracts that learners and teachers have agreed upon and that specify what they agree to accomplish within the course), personal interaction, feelings toward the knower and learner, and the sense of progress and frustration.

Dieter Stroinigg (in Stevick 1980: 185–6) presents a protocol of what a first day's CLL class covered which is outlined here:

1. Informal greetings and self-introductions were made.
2. The teacher made a statement of the goals and guidelines for the course.
3. A conversation session in the foreign language took place.
   a. A circle was formed so that everyone had visual contact with each other and all were within easy reach of a tape recorder microphone.
   b. One student initiated conversation with another student by giving a message in the L1 (English).
   c. The instructor, standing behind the student, whispered a close equivalent of the message in the L2 (German).
   d. The student then repeated the L2 message to its addressee and into the tape recorder microphone as well.
   e. Each student had a chance to compose and record a few messages.
   f. The tape recorder was rewound and replayed at intervals.
   g. Each student repeated the meaning in English of what he or she had said in the L2 and helped to refresh the memory of others.
4. Students then participated in a reflection period, in which they were asked to express their feelings about the previous experience with total frankness.
5. From the material just recorded the instructor chose sentences to write on the blackboard that highlighted elements of grammar, spelling, and peculiarities of capitalization in the L2.
6. Students were encouraged to ask questions about any of the above.
7. Students were encouraged to copy sentences from the board with notes on meaning and usage. This became their "textbook" for home study.

This inventory of activities encompasses the major suggestions for classroom practices appearing in the most recent literature on CLL. Other procedures, however, may emerge fortuitously on the basis of learner–knower interactions in the classroom context.

Conclusion

Community Language Learning is the most responsive of the methods we have reviewed in terms of its sensitivity to learner communicative intent. It should be noted, however, that this communicative intent is constrained by the number and knowledge of fellow learners. A learner's desire to understand or express technical terms used in aeronautical engineering is unlikely to receive adequate response in the CLL class. Community Language Learning places unusual demands on language teachers. They must be highly proficient and sensitive to nuance in both L1 and L2. They must be familiar with and sympathetic to the role of counselors in psychological counseling. They must resist the pressure "to teach" in the traditional senses. As one CLL teacher notes, "I had to relax completely and to exclude my own will to produce something myself. I had to exclude any function of forming or formulating something within me, not trying to *do* something"(Curran 1976: 33).

The teacher must also be relatively nondirective and must be prepared to accept and even encourage the "adolescent" aggression of the learner as he or she strives for independence. The teacher must operate without conventional materials, depending on student topics to shape and motivate the class. In addition, the teacher must be prepared to deal with potentially hostile learner reactions to the method. The teacher must also be culturally sensitive and prepared to redesign the language class into more culturally compatible organizational forms. And the teacher must attempt to learn these new roles and skills without much specific guidance from CLL texts presently available. Special training in Community Language Learning techniques is usually required.

Critics of Community Language Learning question the appropriateness of the counseling metaphor upon which it is predicated, asking for evidence that language learning in classrooms indeed parallels the processes that characterize psychological counseling. Questions also arise about whether teachers should attempt counseling without special training. CLL procedures were largely developed and tested with groups of college-age Americans. The problems and successes experienced by one or two different client groups may not necessarily represent language learning universals. Other concerns have been expressed regarding the lack of a syllabus, which makes objectives unclear and evaluation difficult to accomplish, and the focus on fluency rather than accuracy, which may lead to inadequate control of the grammatical system of the target language. Supporters of CLL, on the other hand, emphasize the positive benefits of a method that centers on the learner and stresses the humanistic side of language learning, and not merely its linguistic dimensions.

Bibliography

Brown, H. D. 1977. Some limitations of C-L/CLL models of second language teaching. *TESOL Quarterly* 11(4): 365–72.

Curran, C.A. 1972. *Counseling-Learning: A Whole-Person Model for Education.* New York: Grune and Stratton.

Curran, C. 1976. *Counseling-Learning in Second Languages.* Apple River, Ill.: Apple River Press.

La Forge. P. G. 1971. Community language learning: a pilot study. *Language Learning* 21(1): 45–61.

La Forge, P. G. 1975. *Research Profiles with Community Language Learning.* Apple River, Ill.: Apple River Press.

La Forge. P. G. 1975. Community language learning: the Japanese case. In F. C. C. Peng. (ed.), *Language in Japanese Society,* pp. 215–46. Tokyo: University of Tokyo Press.

La Forge, P. G. 1977. Uses of social silence in the interpersonal dynamics of Community Language Learning. *TESOL Quarterly* 11(4): 373–82.

La Forge, P. G. 1983. *Counseling and Culture in Second Language Acquisition.* Oxford: Pergamon.

Lim, K. B. 1968. The unified language project. *RELC Journal* 9(1): 19–27.

Mackey, W. F. 1972. *Bilingual Education in a Binational School.* Rowley, Mass.: Newbury House.

Moskowitz, G. 1978. *Caring and Sharing in the Foreign Language Class.* Rowley, Mass.: Newbury House.

Munby, J. 1978. *Communicative Syllabus Design.* Cambridge: Cambridge University Press.

Rardin, J. 1976. A Counseling-Learning model for second language learning. *TESOL Newsletter* 10(2): 21–2.

Rardin, J. 1977. The language teacher as facilitator. *TESOL Quarterly* 11(4): 383–8.

Rogers, C. R. 1951. *Client-Centered Therapy.* Boston: Houghton Mifflin.

Stevick, E. W. 1973. Review article: Charles A. Curran's Counseling-Learning: a whole person model for education. *Language Learning* 23(2): 259–71.

Stevick, E. W. 1976. *Memory, Meaning and Method: Some Psychological Perspectives on Language Learning.* Rowley, Mass.: Newbury House.

Stevick, E. W. 1980. *Teaching Languages: A Way and Ways.* Rowley, Mass.: Newbury House.

Taylor, B. P. 1979. Exploring Community Language Learning. In C. Yorio et al. (eds.), *On TESOL '79,* pp. 80–4. Washington, D.C.: TESOL.

Tranel, D. D. 1968. Teaching Latin with the chromachord. *The Classical Journal* 63: 157–60.

9 The Natural Approach

Background

In 1977, Tracy Terrell, a teacher of Spanish in California, outlined "a proposal for a 'new' philosophy of language teaching which [he] called the Natural Approach" (Terrell 1977; 1982: 121). This was an attempt to develop a language teaching proposal that incorporated the "naturalistic" principles researchers had identified in studies of second language acquisition. The Natural Approach grew out of Terrell's experiences teaching Spanish classes. Since that time Terrell and others have experimented with implementing the Natural Approach in elementary- to advanced-level classes and with several other languages. At the same time he has joined forces with Stephen Krashen, an applied linguist at the University of Southern California, in elaborating a theoretical rationale for the Natural Approach, drawing on Krashen's influential theory of second language acquisition. Krashen and Terrell's combined statement of the principles and practices of the Natural Approach appeared in their book, *The Natural Approach*, published in 1983. The Natural Approach has attracted a wider interest than some of the other innovative language teaching proposals discussed in this book, largely because of its support by Krashen. Krashen and Terrell's book contains theoretical sections prepared by Krashen that outline his views on second language acquisition (Krashen 1981; 1982), and sections on implementation and classroom procedures, prepared largely by Terrell.

Krashen and Terrell have identified the Natural Approach with what they call "traditional" approaches to language teaching. Traditional approaches are defined as "based on the use of language in communicative situations without recourse to the native language" – and, perhaps, needless to say, without reference to grammatical analysis, grammatical drilling, or to a particular theory of grammar. Krashen and Terrell note that such "approaches have been called natural, psychological, phonetic, new, reform, direct, analytic, imitative and so forth" (Krashen and Terrell 1983: 9). The fact that the authors of the Natural Approach relate their approach to the Natural Method (see Chapter 1) has led some to assume that *Natural Approach* and *Natural Method* are synonymous terms. Although the tradition is a common one, there are important differences between the Natural Approach and the older Natural Method, which it will be useful to consider at the outset.

The Natural Method is another term for what by the turn of the century had become known as the Direct Method (see Chapter 1). It is described in a report on the state of the art in language teaching commissioned by the Modern Language Association in 1901 (the report of the "Committee of 12"):

> In its extreme form the method consisted of a series of monologues by the teacher interspersed with exchanges of question and answer between the instructor and the pupil – all in the foreign language... A great deal of pantomime accompanied the talk. With the aid of this gesticulation, by attentive listening and by dint of much repetition the learner came to associate certain acts and objects with certain combinations of the sounds and finally reached the point of reproducing the foreign words or phrases... Not until a considerable familiarity with the spoken word was attained was the scholar allowed to see the foreign language in print. The study of grammar was reserved for a still later period. (Cole 1931: 58)

The term *natural*, used in reference to the Direct Method, merely emphasized that the principles underlying the method were believed to conform to the principles of naturalistic language learning in young children. Similarly, the Natural Approach, as defined by Krashen and Terrell, is believed to conform to the naturalistic principles found in successful second language acquisition. Unlike the Direct Method, however, it places less emphasis on teacher monologues, direct repetition, and formal questions and answers, and less focus on accurate production of target language sentences. In the Natural Approach there is an emphasis on exposure, or *input*, rather than practice; optimizing emotional preparedness for learning; a prolonged period of attention to what the language learners hear before they try to produce language; and a willingness to use written and other materials as a source of comprehensible input. The emphasis on the central role of comprehension in the Natural Approach links it to other comprehension-based approaches in language teaching (see Chapter 6).

Approach

Theory of language

Krashen and Terrell see communication as the primary function of language, and since their approach focuses on teaching communicative abilities, they refer to the Natural Approach as an example of a communicative approach. The Natural Approach "is similar to other communicative approaches being developed today" (Krashen and Terrell 1983: 17). They reject earlier methods of language teaching, such as the Audiolingual Method, which viewed grammar as the central component of language. According to Krashen and Terrell, the major problem with these methods was that they were built not around "actual theories of language acquisition, but theories of something else; for example, the structure of language" (1983: 1). Unlike proponents of Communicative Language Teaching (Chapter 5), however, Krashen and Terrell give little attention to a theory of language. Indeed, a recent critic of Krashen suggests he has no theory of language at all (Gregg 1984). What Krashen and Terrell do describe about the nature of language emphasizes the primacy of meaning. The importance of the vocabulary is stressed, for example, suggesting the view that a language is essentially its lexicon and only inconsequently the grammar that determines how the lexicon is exploited to produce messages. Terrell quotes Dwight Bolinger to support this view:

The quantity of information in the lexicon far outweighs that in any other part of the language, and if there is anything to the notion of redundancy it should be easier to reconstruct a message containing just words than one containing just the syntactic relations. The significant fact is the subordinate role of grammar. The most important thing is to get the words in. (Bolinger, in Terrell 1977: 333).

Language is viewed as a vehicle for communicating meanings and messages. Hence Krashen and Terrell state that "acquisition can take place only when people understand messages in the target language (Krashen and Terrell 1983: 19). Yet despite their avowed communicative approach to language, they view language learning, as do audiolingualists, as mastery of structures by stages. "The input hypothesis states that in order for acquirers to progress to the next stage in the acquisition of the target language, they need to understand input language that includes a structure that is part of the next stage" (Krashen and Terrell 1983: 32). Krashen refers to this with the formula "I + 1" (i.e., input that contains structures slightly above the learner's present level). We assume that Krashen means by *structures* something at least in the tradition of what such linguists as Leonard Bloomfield and Charles Fries meant by *structures*. The Natural Approach thus assumes a linguistic hierarchy of structural complexity that one masters through encounters with "input" containing structures at the "I + 1" level.

We are left then with a view of language that consists of lexical items, structures, and messages. Obviously, there is no particular novelty in this view as such, except that messages are considered of primary importance in the Natural Approach. The lexicon for both perception and production is considered critical in the construction and interpretation of messages. Lexical items in messages are necessarily grammatically structured, and more complex messages involve more complex grammatical structure. Although they acknowledge such grammatical structuring, Krashen and Terrell feel that grammatical structure does not require explicit analysis or attention by the language teacher, by the language learner, or in language teaching materials.

Theory of learning

Krashen and Terrell make continuing reference to the theoretical and research base claimed to underlie the Natural Approach and to the fact that the method is unique in having such a base. "It is based on an empirically grounded theory of second language acquisition, which has been supported by a large number of scientific studies in a wide variety of language acquisition and learning contexts" (Krashen and Terrell 1983: 1). The theory and research are grounded on Krashen's views of language acquisition, which we will collectively refer to as Krashen's language acquisition theory. Krashen's views have been presented and discussed extensively elsewhere (e.g., Krashen 1982), so we will not try to present or critique Krashen's arguments here. (For a detailed critical review, see Gregg 1984 and McLaughlin 1978). It is necessary, however, to present in outline form the principal tenets of the theory, since it is on these that the design and procedures in the Natural Approach are based.

THE ACQUISITION/LEARNING HYPOTHESIS

The Acquisition/Learning Hypothesis claims that there are two distinctive ways of developing competence in a second or foreign language. *Acquisition* is the "natural" way, paralleling first language development in children. Acquisition refers to an unconscious process that involves the naturalistic development of language proficiency through understanding language and through using language for meaningful communication. *Learning*, by contrast, refers to a process in which conscious rules about a language are developed. It results in explicit knowledge about the forms of a language and the ability to verbalize this knowledge. Formal teaching is necessary for "learning" to occur, and correction of errors helps with the development of learned rules. Learning, according to the theory, cannot lead to acquisition.

THE MONITOR HYPOTHESIS

The acquired linguistic system is said to initiate utterances when we communicate in a second or foreign language. Conscious learning can function only as a monitor or editor that checks and repairs the output

131

of the acquired system. The Monitor Hypothesis claims that we may call upon learned knowledge to correct ourselves when we communicate, but that conscious learning (i.e., the *learned* system) has *only* this function. Three conditions limit the successful use of the monitor:

1. *Time.* There must be sufficient time for a learner to choose and apply a learned rule.
2. *Focus on form.* The language user must be focused on correctness or on the form of the output.
3. *Knowledge of rules.* The performer must know the rules. The monitor does best with rules that are simple in two ways. They must be simple to describe and they must not require complex movements and rearrangements.

THE NATURAL ORDER HYPOTHESIS

According to the Natural Order Hypothesis, the acquisition of grammatical structures proceeds in a predictable order. Research is said to have shown that certain grammatical structures or morphemes are acquired before others in first language acquisition of English, and a similar natural order is found in second language acquisition. Errors are signs of naturalistic developmental processes, and during acquisition (but not during learning), similar developmental errors occur in learners no matter what their mother tongue is.

THE INPUT HYPOTHESIS

The Input Hypothesis claims to explain the relationship between what the learner is exposed to of a language (the input) and language acquisition. It involves four main issues.

First, the hypothesis relates to acquisition, and not to learning.

Second, people acquire language best by understanding input that is slightly beyond their current level of competence:

An acquirer can "move" from a stage I (where I is the acquirer's level of competence) to a stage I + 1 (where I + 1 is the stage immediately following I along some natural order) by understanding language containing I + 1. (Krashen and Terrell 1983: 32)

Clues based on the situation and the context, extralinguistic information, and knowledge of the world make comprehension possible.

Third, the ability to speak fluently cannot be taught directly; rather, it "emerges" independently in time, after the acquirer has built up linguistic competence by understanding input.

Fourth, if there is a sufficient quantity of comprehensible input, I + 1 will usually be provided automatically. Comprehensible input refers to utterances that the learner understands based on the context in which they are used as well as the language in which they are phrased. When a speaker uses language so that the acquirer understands the message, the speaker "casts a net" of structure around the acquirer's current level of competence, and this will include many instances of I + 1. Thus, input need not be finely tuned to a learner's current level of linguistic competence, and in fact cannot be so finely tuned in a language class, where learners will be at many different levels of competence.

Just as child acquirers of a first language are provided with samples of "caretaker speech," rough-tuned to their present level of understanding, so adult acquirers of a second language are provided with simple codes that facilitate second language comprehension. One such code is "foreigner talk," which refers to the speech native speakers use to simplify communication with foreigners. Foreigner talk is characterized by a slower rate of speech, repetition, restating, use of Yes/No instead of Wh- questions, and other changes that make messages more comprehensible to persons of limited language proficiency.

THE AFFECTIVE FILTER HYPOTHESIS

Krashen sees the learner's emotional state or attitudes as an adjustable filter that freely passes, impedes, or blocks input necessary to acquisition. A low affective filter is desirable, since it impedes or blocks less of this necessary input. The hypothesis is built on research in second language acquisition, which has identified three kinds of affective or attitudinal variables related to second language acquisition.

1. *Motivation.* Learners with high motivation generally do better.
2. *Self-confidence.* Learners with self-confidence and a good self-image tend to be more successful.
3. *Anxiety.* Low personal anxiety and low classroom anxiety are more conducive to second language acquisition.

The Affective Filter Hypothesis states that acquirers with a low affective filter seek and receive more input, interact with confidence, and are more receptive to the input they receive. Anxious acquirers have a high affective filter, which prevents acquisition from taking place. It is believed that the affective filter (e.g., fear or embarrassment) rises in early adolescence, and this may account for children's apparent superiority to older acquirers of a second language.

These five hypotheses have obvious implications for language teaching. In sum, these are:

1. As much comprehensible input as possible must be presented.
2. Whatever helps comprehension is important. Visual aids are useful, as is exposure to a wide range of vocabulary rather than study of syntactic structure.

133

3. The focus in the classroom should be on listening and reading; speaking should be allowed to "emerge."
4. In order to lower the affective filter, student work should center on meaningful communication rather than on form; input should be interesting and so contribute to a relaxed classroom atmosphere.

Design

Objectives

The Natural Approach "is for beginners and is designed to help them become intermediates." It has the expectation that students

will be able to function adequately in the target situation. They will understand the speaker of the target language (perhaps with requests for clarification), and will be able to convey (in a non-insulting manner) their requests and ideas. They need not know every word in a particular semantic domain, nor is it necessary that the syntax and vocabulary be flawless—but their production does need to be understood. They should be able to make the meaning clear but not necessarily be accurate in all details of grammar. (Krashen and Terrell 1983: 71)

However, since the Natural Approach is offered as a general set of principles applicable to a wide variety of situations, as in Communicative Language Teaching, specific objectives depend upon learner needs and the skill (reading, writing, listening, or speaking) and level being taught.

Krashen and Terrell feel it is important to communicate to learners what they can expect of a course as well as what they should not expect. They offer as an example a possible goal and nongoal statement for a beginning Natural Approach Spanish class.

After 100–150 hours of Natural Approach Spanish, you *will* be able to: "get around" in Spanish; you will be able to communicate with a monolingual native speaker of Spanish without difficulty; read most ordinary texts in Spanish with some use of a dictionary; know enough Spanish to continue to improve on your own.

After 100–150 hours of Natural Approach Spanish you will *not* be able to: pass for a native speaker, use Spanish as easily as you use English, understand native speakers when they talk to each other (you will probably not be able to eavesdrop successfully); use Spanish on the telephone with great comfort; participate easily in a conversation with several other native speakers on unfamiliar topics. (Krashen and Terrell 1983: 74).

The syllabus

Krashen and Terrell (1983) approach course organization from two points of view. First, they list some typical goals for language courses and suggest which of these goals are the ones at which the Natural Approach aims. They list such goals under four areas:

1. Basic personal communication skills: oral (e.g., listening to announcements in public places)
2. Basic personal communication skills: written (e.g., reading and writing personal letters)
3. Academic learning skills: oral (e.g., listening to a lecture)
4. Academic learning skills: written (e.g., taking notes in class)

Of these, they note that the Natural Approach is primarily "designed to develop basic communication skills – both oral and written (1983: 67). They then observe that communication goals "may be expressed in terms of situations, functions and topics" and proceed to order four pages of topics and situations "which are likely to be most useful to beginning students" (1983: 67). The functions are not specified or suggested but are felt to derive naturally from the topics and situations. This approach to syllabus design would appear to derive to some extent from threshold level specifications (see Chapter 5).

The second point of view holds that "the purpose of a language course will vary according to the needs of the students and their particular interests" (Krashen and Terrell 1983: 65).

The goals of a Natural Approach class are based on an assessment of student needs. We determine the situations in which they will use the target language and the sorts of topics they will have to communicate information about. In setting communication goals, we do not expect the students at the end of a particular course to have acquired a certain group of structures or forms. Instead we expect them to deal with a particular set of topics in a given situation. We do not organize the activities of the class about a grammatical syllabus. (Krashen and Terrell 1983:71)

From this point of view it is difficult to specify communicative goals that necessarily fit the needs of all students. Thus any list of topics and situations must be understood as syllabus suggestions rather than as specifications.

As well as fitting the needs and interests of students, content selection should aim to create a low affective filter by being interesting and fostering a friendly, relaxed atmosphere, should provide a wide exposure to vocabulary that may be useful to basic personal communication, and should resist any focus on grammatical structures, since if input is provided "over a wider variety of topics while pursuing communicative goals, the necessary grammatical structures are automatically provided in the input" (Krashen and Terrell 1983: 71).

Types of learning and teaching activities

From the beginning of a class taught according to the Natural Approach, emphasis is on presenting comprehensible input in the target language. Teacher talk focuses on objects in the classroom and on the content of pictures, as with the Direct Method. To minimize stress, learners are not required to say anything until they feel ready, but they are expected to respond to teacher commands and questions in other ways.

When learners are ready to begin talking in the new language, the teacher provides comprehensible language and simple response opportunities. The teacher talks slowly and distinctly, asking questions and eliciting one-word answers. There is a gradual progression from Yes/No questions, through either-or questions, to questions that students can answer using words they have heard used by the teacher. Students are not expected to use a word actively until they have heard it many times. Charts, pictures, advertisements, and other realia serve as the focal point for questions, and when the students' competence permits, talk moves to class members. "Acquisition activities" – those that focus on meaningful communication rather than language form – are emphasized. Pair or group work may be employed, followed by whole-class discussion led by the teacher.

Techniques recommended by Krashen and Terrell are often borrowed from other methods and adapted to meet the requirements of Natural Approach theory. These include command-based activities from Total Physical Response; Direct Method activities in which mime, gesture, and context are used to elicit questions and answers; and even situation-based practice of structures and patterns. Group-work activities are often identical to those used in Communicative Language Teaching, where sharing information in order to complete a task is emphasized. There is nothing novel about the procedures and techniques advocated for use with the Natural Approach. A casual observer might not be aware of the philosophy underlying the classroom techniques he or she observes. What characterizes the Natural Approach is the use of familiar techniques within the framework of a method that focuses on providing comprehensible input and a classroom environment that cues comprehension of input, minimizes learner anxiety, and maximizes learner self-confidence.

Learner roles

There is a basic assumption in the Natural Approach that learners should not try to learn a language in the usual sense. The extent to which they can lose themselves in activities involving meaningful communication will determine the amount and kind of acquisition they will experience and the fluency they will ultimately demonstrate. The language acquirer is seen as a processor of comprehensible input. The acquirer is challenged by input that is slightly beyond his or her current level of competence and is able to assign meaning to this input through active use of context and extralinguistic information.

Learners' roles are seen to change according to their stage of linguistic development. Central to these changing roles are learner decisions on when to speak, what to speak about, and what linguistic expressions to use in speaking.

In the *pre-production stage* students "participate in the language activity without having to respond in the target language" (Krashen and Terrell 1983: 76). For example, students can act out physical commands, identify student colleagues from teacher description, point to pictures, and so forth.

In the *early-production stage*, students respond to either-or questions, use single words and short phrases, fill in charts, and use fixed conversational patterns (e.g., How are you? What's your name?).

In the *speech-emergent phase*, students involve themselves in role play and games, contribute personal information and opinions, and participate in group problem solving.

Learners have four kinds of responsibilities in the Natural Approach classroom:

1. Provide information about their specific goals so that acquisition activities can focus on the topics and situations most relevant to their needs.
2. Take an active role in ensuring comprehensible input. They should learn and use conversational management techniques to regulate input.
3. Decide when to start producing speech and when to upgrade it.
4. Where learning exercises (i.e., grammar study) are to be a part of the program, decide with the teacher the relative amount of time to be devoted to them and perhaps even complete and correct them independently.

Learners are expected to participate in communication activities with other learners. Although communication activities are seen to provide naturalistic practice and to create a sense of camaraderie, which lowers the affective filter, they may fail to provide learners with well-formed and comprehensible input at the I + 1 level. Krashen and Terrell warn of these shortcomings but do not suggest means for their amelioration.

Teacher roles

The Natural Approach teacher has three central roles. First, the teacher is the primary source of comprehensible input in the target language. "Class time is devoted primarily to providing input for acquisition," and the teacher is the primary generator of that input. In this role the teacher is required to generate a constant flow of language input while providing a multiplicity of nonlinguistic clues to assist students in interpreting the input. The Natural Approach demands a much more center-stage role for the teacher than do many contemporary communicative methods.

Second, the Natural Approach teacher creates a classroom atmosphere that is interesting, friendly, and in which there is a low affective filter for learning. This is achieved in part through such Natural Approach techniques as not demanding speech from the students before they are ready for it, not correcting student errors, and providing subject matter of high interest to students.

Finally, the teacher must choose and orchestrate a rich mix of classroom activities, involving a variety of group sizes, content, and contexts. The teacher is seen as responsible for collecting materials and designing their use. These materials, according to Krashen and Terrell, are based not just on teacher perceptions but on elicited student needs and interests.

As with other nonorthodox teaching systems, the Natural Approach teacher has a particular responsibility to communicate clearly and compellingly to students the assumptions, organization, and expectations of the method, since in many cases these will violate student views of what language learning and teaching are supposed to be.

The role of instructional materials

The primary goal of materials in the Natural Approach is to make classroom activities as meaningful as possible by supplying "the extralinguistic context that helps the acquirer to understand and thereby to acquire" (Krashen and Terrell 1983: 55), by relating classroom activities to the real world, and by fostering real communication among the learners. Materials come from the world of realia rather than from textbooks. The primary aim of materials is to promote comprehension and communication. Pictures and other visual aids are essential, because they supply the content for communication. They facilitate the acquisition of a large vocabulary within the classroom. Other recommended materials include schedules, brochures, advertisements, maps, and books at levels appropriate to the students, if a reading component is included in the course. Games, in general, are seen as useful classroom materials, since "games by their very nature, focus the student on what it is they are doing and use the language as a tool for reaching the goal rather than as a goal in itself" (Terrell 1982: 121). The selection, reproduction, and collection of materials places a considerable burden on the Natural Approach teacher. Since Krashen and Terrell suggest a syllabus of topics and situations, it is likely that at some point collections of materials to supplement teacher presentations will be published, built around the "syllabus" of topics and situations recommended by the Natural Approach.

Procedure

We have seen that the Natural Approach adopts techniques and activities freely from various method sources and can be regarded as innovative only with respect to the purposes for which they are recommended and the ways they are used. Krashen and Terrell (1983) provide suggestions for the use of a wide range of activities, all of which are familiar components of Situational Language Teaching, Communicative Language Teaching, and other methods discussed in this book. To illustrate procedural aspects of the Natural Approach, we will cite examples of how such activities are to be used in the Natural Approach classroom to provide comprehensible input, without requiring production of responses or minimal responses in the target language.

1. Start with TPR [Total Physical Response] commands. At first the commands are quite simple: "Stand up. Turn around. Raise your right hand."
2. Use TPR to teach names of body parts and to introduce numbers and sequence. "Lay your right hand on your head, put both hands on your shoulder, first touch your nose, then stand up and turn to the right three times" and so forth.
3. Introduce classroom terms and props into commands. "Pick up a pencil and put it under the book, touch a wall, go to the door and knock three times." Any item which can be brought to the class can be incorporated. "Pick up the record and place it in the tray. Take the green blanket to Larry. Pick up the soap and take it to the woman wearing the green blouse."
4. Use names of physical characteristics and clothing to identify members of the class by name. The instructor uses context and the items themselves to make the meanings of the key words clear: hair, long, short, etc. Then a student is described. "What is your name?" (selecting a student). "Class. Look at Barbara. She has long brown hair. Her hair is long and brown. Her hair is not short. It is long." (Using mime, pointing and context to ensure comprehension). "What's the name of the student with long brown hair?" (Barbara). Questions such as "What is the name of the woman with the short blond hair?" or "What is the name of the student sitting next to the man with short brown hair and glasses?" are very simple to understand by attending to key words, gestures and context. And they require the students only to remember and produce the name of a fellow student. The same can be done with articles of clothing and colors. "Who is wearing a yellow shirt? Who is wearing a brown dress?"
5. Use visuals, typically magazine pictures, to introduce new vocabulary and to continue with activities requiring only student names as response. The instructor introduces the pictures to the entire class one at a time focusing

usually on one single item or activity in the picture. He may introduce one to five new words while talking about the picture. He then passes the picture to a particular student in the class. The students' task is to remember the name of the student with a particular picture. For example, "Tom has the picture of the sailboat. Joan has the picture of the family watching television" and so forth. The instructor will ask questions like "Who has the picture with the sailboat? Does Susan or Tom have the picture of the people on the beach?" Again the students need only produce a name in response.

6. Combine use of pictures with TPR. "Jim, find the picture of the little girl with her dog and give it to the woman with the pink blouse."
7. Combine observations about the pictures with commands and conditionals. "If there is a woman in your picture, stand up. If there is something blue in your picture, touch your right shoulder."
8. Using several pictures, ask students to point to the picture being described. Picture 1. "There are several people in this picture. One appears to be a father, the other a daughter. What are they doing? Cooking. They are cooking a hamburger." Picture 2. "There are two men in this picture. They are young. They are boxing." Picture 3 . . .

(Krashen and Terrell 1983: 75–7)

In all these activities, the instructor maintains a constant flow of "comprehensible input," using key vocabulary items, appropriate gestures, context, repetition, and paraphrase to ensure the comprehensibility of the input.

Conclusion

The Natural Approach belongs to a tradition of language teaching methods based on observation and interpretation of how learners acquire both first and second languages in nonformal settings. Such methods reject the formal (grammatical) organization of language as a prerequisite to teaching. They hold with Newmark and Reibel that "an adult can effectively be taught by grammatically unordered materials" and that such an approach is, indeed, "the *only* learning process which we know for certain will produce mastery of the language at a native level" (1968: 153). In the Natural Approach, a focus on comprehension and meaningful communication as well as the provision of the right kinds of comprehensible input provide the necessary and sufficient conditions for successful classroom second and foreign language acquisition. This has led to a new rationale for the integration and adaptation of techniques drawn from a wide variety of existing sources. Like Communicative Language Teaching, the Natural Approach is hence evolutionary rather than revolutionary in its procedures. Its greatest claim to originality lies not in the techniques it employs but in their use in a method that emphasizes comprehensible and meaningful practice activities, rather than production of grammatically perfect utterances and sentences.

Bibliography

Cole, R. 1931. *Modern Foreign Languages and Their Teaching.* New York: Appleton-Century-Crofts.

Gregg, K. 1984. Krashen's monitor and Occam's razor. *Applied Linguistics* 5(2): 79–100.

Krashen, S. 1981. *Second Language Acquisition and Second Language Learning.* Oxford: Pergamon.

Krashen, S. 1982. *Principles and Practices in Second Language Acquisition.* Oxford: Pergamon.

Krashen, S. D., and T. D. Terrell. 1983. *The Natural Approach: Language Acquisition in the Classroom.* Oxford: Pergamon.

McLaughlin, B. 1978. The Monitor Model: some methodological considerations. *Language Learning* 28(2): 309–32.

Newmark, L., and Reibel, D. A. 1968. Necessity and sufficiency in language learning. *International Review of Applied Linguistics* 6(2): 145–64.

Rivers, W. 1981. *Teaching Foreign-language Skills.* 2nd ed. Chicago: University of Chicago Press.

Stevick, E. W. 1976. *Memory, Meaning and Method: Some Psychological Perspectives on Language Learning.* Rowley, Mass.: Newbury House.

Terrell, T. D. 1977. A natural approach to second language acquisition and learning. *Modern Language Journal* 61: 325–36.

Terrell, T. D. 1981. The natural approach in bilingual education. Ms. California Office of Bilingual Education.

Terrell, T. D. 1982. The natural approach to language teaching: an update. *Modern Language Journal* 66: 121–32.

10 Suggestopedia

Background

Suggestopedia is a method developed by the Bulgarian psychiatrist-educator Georgi Lozanov. Suggestopedia is a specific set of learning recommendations derived from Suggestology, which Lozanov describes as a "science ... concerned with the systematic study of the nonrational and/or nonconscious influences" that human beings are constantly responding to (Stevick 1976: 42). Suggestopedia tries to harness these influences and redirect them so as to optimize learning. The most conspicuous characteristics of Suggestopedia are the decoration, furniture, and arrangement of the classroom, the use of music, and the authoritative behavior of the teacher. The method has a somewhat mystical air about it, partially because it has few direct links with established learning or educational theory in the West, and partially because of its arcane terminology and neologisms, which one critic has unkindly called a "package of pseudo-scientific gobbledygook" (Scovel 1979: 258).

The claims for suggestopedic learning are dramatic. "There is no sector of public life where suggestology would not be useful" (Lozanov 1978: 2). "Memorization in learning by the suggestopedic method seems to be accelerated 25 times over that in learning by conventional methods" (Lozanov 1978: 27). Precise descriptions of the conditions under which Suggestopedia experiments were run are as hard to come by as are precise descriptions of "successful" classroom procedures. For example, Earl Stevick, a generally enthusiastic supporter of Suggestopedia, notes that Suggestopedia teachers are trained to read dialogues in a special way. "The precise ways of using voice quality, intonation, and timing are apparently both important and intricate. I have found no one who could give a first-hand account of them" (Stevick 1976: 157).

Lozanov acknowledges ties in tradition to yoga and Soviet psychology. From raja-yoga, Lozanov has borrowed and modified techniques for altering states of consciousness and concentration, and the use of rhythmic breathing. From Soviet psychology Lozanov has taken the notion that all students can be taught a given subject matter at the same level of skill. Lozanov claims that his method works equally well whether or not students spend time on outside study. He promises success through Suggestopedia to the academically gifted and ungifted alike. Soviet psy-

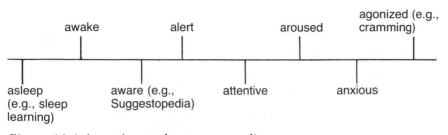

Figure 10.1 Attention and memory studies

chology also stresses the learning environment, and Lozanov similarly specifies the requirements of an optimal learning environment in great detail. (For an overview of the tenets of Soviet psychology and how these differ from those of Western psychology, see Bancroft 1978).

Suggestopedia can perhaps be best understood as one of a range of theories that purport to describe how attentiveness is manipulated to optimize learning and recall. A number of researchers have attempted to identify the optimal mental states for facilitating memorization and facilitating recall. The continuum in Figure 10.1 displays labels for various states of attention that have been examined for their facilitation of inhibition of memorization. The point at the far left represents studies of sleep learning. The point at the far right represents studies on the efficiency of cramming. Lozanov believes most learning takes place in a relaxed but focused state. We thus locate Lozanov's proposals in the aware–alert area.

A most conspicuous feature of Suggestopedia is the centrality of music and musical rhythm to learning. Suggestopedia thus has a kinship with other functional uses of music, particularly therapy. One of the earliest attested uses of music therapy is recorded in the Old Testament of the Bible: "When the evil spirit from God was upon Saul, David took up his harp and played with his hand; so Saul found relief; and it was well with him, and the evil spirit departed from him" (1 Samuel 12:23). Lozanov might have described this incident as the use of music to assist in the "liberation from discrete micro psychotraumata, for destruction of incompatible ideas about the limits of human capabilities" (Lozanov 1978: 252).

Gaston (1968) defines three functions of music in therapy: to facilitate the establishment and maintenance of personal relations; to bring about increased self-esteem through increased self-satisfaction in musical performance; and to use the unique potential of rhythm to energize and bring order. This last function seems to be the one that Lozanov calls upon in his use of music to relax learners as well as to structure, pace, and punctuate the presentation of linguistic material.

Approach

Theory of language

Lozanov does not articulate a theory of language, nor does it seem he is much concerned with any particular assumptions regarding language elements and their organization. The emphasis on memorization of vocabulary pairs – a target language item and its native language translation – suggests a view of language in which lexis is central and in which lexical translation rather than contextualization is stressed. However, Lozanov does occasionally refer to the importance of experiencing language material in "whole meaningful texts" (Lozanov 1978: 268) and notes that the suggestopedic course directs "the student not to vocabulary memorization and acquiring habits of speech, but to acts of communication" (1978: 109).

Lozanov recommends home study of recordings of "whole meaningful texts (not of a fragmentary nature)" that are, "above all, interesting." These are listened to "for the sake of the music of the foreign speech" (Lozanov 1978: 277). The texts should be lighthearted stories with emotional content. Lozanov's recommendations of such stories seems to be entirely motivational, however, and does not represent a commitment to the view that language is preeminently learned for and used in its emotive function.

In describing course work and text organization Lozanov refers most often to the language to be learned as "the material" (e.g., "The new material that is to be learned is read or recited by a well-trained teacher") (Lozanov 1978: 270). One feels that the linguistic nature of the material is largely irrelevant and that if the focus of a language course were, say, memorization of grammar rules, Lozanov would feel a suggestopedic approach to be the optimal one. The sample protocol given for an Italian lesson (Lozanov 1978) does not suggest a theory of language markedly different from that which holds a language to be its vocabulary and the grammar rules for organizing vocabulary.

Theory of learning

Suggestion is at the heart of Suggestopedia. To many, *suggestion* conjures up visions of the penetrating stare, swinging cat's eye, and monotonically repeated injunctions of the hypnotist. Lozanov acknowledges the likelihood of this association to Suggestopedia but claims that his own views separate Suggestopedia from the "narrow clinical concept of hypnosis as a kind of static, sleep like, altered state of consciousness" (1978: 3). Lozanov further claims that what distinguishes his method from hypnosis and other forms of mind control is that these other forms lack "a desuggestive-suggestive sense" and "fail to create a constant set up to reserves through concentrative psycho-relaxation" (1978: 267). (We intrepret *reserves* as being something like human memory banks. *Desuggestion* seems to involve unloading the memory banks, or reserves, of unwanted or blocking memories. *Suggestion*, then, involves loading the memory banks with desired and facilitating memories.) There are six principal theoretical components through which desuggestion and suggestion operate and that set up access to reserves. We will describe these briefly following Bancroft (1972).

AUTHORITY

People remember best and are most influenced by information coming from an authoritative source. Lozanov dictates a variety of prescriptions and proscriptions aimed at having Suggestopedia students experience the educational establishment and the teacher as sources having great authority. Lozanov talks of choosing a "ritual placebo system" that is most likely to be perceived of by students as having high authority (Lozanov 1978: 267). Lozanov appears to believe that scientific-sounding language, highly positive experimental data, and true-believer teachers constitute a ritual placebo system that is authoritatively appealing to most learners. Well-publicized accounts of learning success lend the method and the institution authority, and commitment to the method, self-confidence, personal distance, acting ability, and a highly positive attitude give an authoritative air to the teacher.

INFANTILIZATION

Authority is also used to suggest a teacher–student relation like that of parent to child. In the child's role the learner takes part in role playing, games, songs, and gymnastic exercises that help "the older student regain the self-confidence, spontaneity and receptivity of the child" (Bancroft 1972: 19).

DOUBLE-PLANEDNESS

The learner learns not only from the effect of direct instruction but from the environment in which the instruction takes place. The bright decor of the classroom, the musical background, the shape of the chairs, and the personality of the teacher are considered as important in instruction as the form of the instructional material itself.

INTONATION, RHYTHM, AND CONCERT PSEUDO-PASSIVENESS

Varying the tone and rhythm of presented material helps both to avoid boredom through monotony of repetition and to dramatize, emotionalize, and give meaning to linguistic material. In the first presentation of linguistic material three phrases are read together, each with a different voice level and rhythm. In the second presentation the linguistic material is given a proper dramatic reading, which helps learners visualize a context for the material and aids in memorization (Bancroft 1972: 19).

Both intonation and rhythm are coordinated with a musical background. The musical background helps to induce a relaxed attitude, which Lozanov refers to as concert pseudo-passiveness. This state is felt to be optimal for learning, in that anxieties and tension are relieved and power of concentration for new material is raised. Because the role of music is central in suggestopedic learning, it needs to be considered in somewhat more detail.

The type of music is critical to learning success. "The idea that music can affect your body and mind certainly isn't new. . . . The key was to find the right kind of music for just the right kind of effect. . . . The music you use in superlearning [the American term for Suggestopedia] is extremely important. If it does not have the required pattern, the desired altered states of consciousness will not be induced and results will be poor. . . . It is specific music – sonic patterns – for a specific purpose (Ostrander, Schroeder, and Ostrander 1979: 73–4). At the institute Lozanov recommends a series of slow movements (sixty beats a minute) in 4/4 time for Baroque concertos strung together into about a half-hour concert. He notes that in such concerts "the body relaxed, the mind became alert" (Ostrander et al. 1979: 74). As a further refinement, "East German researchers of Suggestopedia at Karl Marx University in Leipzig observed that slow movements from Baroque instrumental music featuring string instruments gave the very best results" (Ostrander et al. 1979: 115).

The rate of presentation of material to be learned within the rhythmic pattern is keyed to the rhythm. Superlearning uses an eight-second cycle for pacing out data at slow intervals. During the first four beats of the cycle there is silence. During the second four beats the teacher presents the material. Ostrander et al. present a variety of evidence on why this pacing to Baroque largo music is so potent. They note that musical rhythms affect body rhythms, such as heartbeat, and that researchers have noted that "with a slow heartbeat, mind efficiency takes a great leap forward" (1979: 63). They cite experimental data such as those which show disastrous learning results when the music of Wagner was substituted for slow Baroque. They reflect that "the minute is divided into sixty seconds and that perhaps there's more to this than just an arbitrary division of time." They further report that "the Indian vilambita, for instance, has the required rhythms of sixty beats a minute" and suggest that Indian yogis may have built the sixty-beat rhythm into yogic techniques. Finally, they observe that not only human but vegetable subjects thrive under sixty-beat stimulation. "Plants grown in the chambers given Baroque music by Bach and Indian music by Ravi Shankar rapidly grew lush and abundant... the plants in the chamber getting rock music shriveled and died" (1979: 82). Suggestopedic learning is consequently built on a particular type of music and a particular rate of presentation.

Design

Objectives

Suggestopedia aims to deliver advanced conversational proficiency quickly. It apparently bases its learning claims on student mastery of prodigious lists of vocabulary pairs and, indeed, suggests to the students that it is appropriate that they set such goals for themselves. Lozanov emphasizes, however, that increased memory power is not an isolated skill but is a result of "positive, comprehensive stimulation of personality" (Lozanov 1978: 253). Lozanov states categorically, "The main aim of teaching is not memorization, but the understanding and creative solution of problems" (1978: 251). As learner goals he cites increased access to understanding and creative solutions of problems. However, because students and teachers place a high value on vocabulary recall, memorization of vocabulary pairs continues to be seen as an important goal of the suggestopedic method.

The syllabus

A Suggestopedia course lasts thirty days and consists of ten units of study. Classes are held four hours a day, six days a week. The central focus of each unit is a dialogue consisting of 1,200 words or so, with an accompanying vocabulary list and grammatical commentary. The dialogues are graded by lexis and grammar.

There is a pattern of work within each unit and a pattern of work for the whole course. Unit study is organized around three days: day 1 – half a day, day 2 – full day, day 3 – half a day. On the first day of work on a new unit the teacher discusses the general content (not structure) of the unit dialogue. The learners then receive the printed dialogue with a native language translation in a parallel column. The teacher answers any questions of interest or concern about the dialogue. The dialogue then is read a second and third time in ways to be discussed subsequently. This is the work for day 1. Days 2 and 3 are spent in primary and secondary elaboration of the text. Primary elaboration consists of imitation, question and answer, reading, and so on, of the dialogue and of working with the 150 new vocabulary items presented in the unit. The secondary elaboration involves encouraging students to make new combinations and productions based on the dialogues. A story or essay paralleling the dialogue is also read. The students engage in conversation and take small roles in response to the text read.

The whole course also has a pattern of presentation and performance. On the first day a test is given to check the level of student knowledge and to provide a basis for dividing students into two groups – one of new beginners and one of modified (false) beginners. The teacher then briefs the students on the course and explains the attitude they should take toward it. This briefing is designed to put them in a positive, relaxed and confident mood for learning. Students are given a new name in the second language and a new biography in the second culture with which they are to operate for the duration of the course.

During the course there are two opportunities for generalization of material. In the middle of the course students are encouraged to practice the target language in a setting where it might be used, such as hotels or restaurants. The last day of the course is devoted to a performance in which every student participates. The students construct a play built on the material of the course. Rules and parts are planned, but students are expected to speak *ex tempore* rather than from memorized lines. Written tests are also given throughout the course, and these and the performance are reviewed on the final day of the course.

Types of learning and teaching activities

We have mentioned a variety of activities in passing in the discussion of the syllabus. These include imitation, question and answer, and role play – which are not activities "that other language teachers would consider to be out of the ordinary" (Stevick 1976: 157). The type of activities that are more original to Suggestopedia are the listening activities, which concern the text and text vocabulary of each unit. These activities are typically part of the "pre-session phase," which takes place on the first day of a new unit. The students first look at and discuss a new text with the teacher. In the second reading, students relax comfortably in reclining chairs and listen to the teacher read the text in a certain way. The quote from Stevick at the beginning of this chapter suggests that the exact nature of the "special way" is not clear. Bancroft notes that the material is "presented with varying intonations and a coordination of sound and printed word or illustration" (Bancroft 1972: 17). During the third reading the material is acted out by the instructor in a dramatic manner over a background of the special musical form described previously. During this phase students lean back in their chairs and breathe deeply and regularly as instructed by the teacher. This is the point at which Lozanov believes the unconscious learning system takes over.

Learner roles

Students volunteer for a suggestopedic course, but having volunteered, they are expected to be committed to the class and its activities. Smoking and drinking are prohibited or discouraged in class and around the school during the course.

The mental state of the learners is critical to success, which is why learners must forgo mind-altering substances and other distractions and immerse themselves in the procedures of the method. Learners must not try to figure out, manipulate, or study the material presented but must maintain a pseudo-passive state, in which the material rolls over and through them.

Students are expected to tolerate and in fact encourage their own "infantilization." In part this is accomplished by acknowledging the absolute authority of the teacher and in part by giving themselves over to activities and techniques designed to help them regain the self-confidence, spontaneity, and receptivity of the child. Such activities include role playing, games, songs, and gymnastic exercises (Bancroft 1972: 19). To assist them in the role plays and to help them detach themselves from their past learning experiences, students are given a new name and personal history within the target culture. The new names also contain phonemes from the target culture that learners find difficult to pronounce. For example, a student of English might be "the *a*ctress Anne M*a*ckey from K*a*nsas."

Groups of learners are ideally socially homogeneous, twelve in number, and divided equally between men and women. Learners sit in a circle, which encourages face-to-face exchange and activity participation.

Teacher roles

The primary role of the teacher is to create situations in which the learner is most suggestible and then to present linguisitic material in a way most likely to encourage positive reception and retention by the learner.

Lozanov lists several expected teacher behaviors that contribute to these presentations.

1. Show absolute confidence in the method.
2. Display fastidious conduct in manners and dress.
3. Organize properly and strictly observe the initial stages of the teaching process – this includes choice and play of music, as well as punctuality.
4. Maintain a solemn attitude towards the session.

5. Give tests and respond tactfully to poor papers (if any).
6. Stress global rather than analytical attitudes towards material.
7. Maintain a modest enthusiasm.

(Lozanov 1978: 275–6)

As Stevick (1976) points out, there are certain styles of presentation of material that are important, intricate, and inaccessible. It appears that teachers have to be prepared to be initiated into the method by stages and that certain techniques are withheld until such times as the master teacher feels the initiate is ready. In addition, Bancroft (1972) suggests that teachers are expected to be skilled in acting, singing, and psychotherapeutic techniques and that a Lozanov-taught teacher will spend three to six months training in these fields.

The role of instructional materials

Materials consist of direct support materials, primarily text and tape, and indirect support materials, including classroom fixtures and music.

The text is organized around the ten units described earlier. The textbook should have emotional force, literary quality, and interesting characters. Language problems should be introduced in a way that does not worry or distract students from the content. "Traumatic themes and distasteful lexical material should be avoided" (Lozanov 1978: 278). Each unit should be governed by a single idea featuring a variety of subthemes, "the way it is in life" (p. 278).

Although not language materials per se, the learning environment plays such a central role in Suggestopedia that the important elements of the environment need to be briefly enumerated. The environment (the indirect support materials) comprises the appearance of the classroom (bright and cheery), the furniture (reclining chairs arranged in a circle), and the music (Baroque largo, selected for reasons discussed previously).

Procedure

As with other methods we have examined, there are variants both historical and individual in the actual conduct of Suggestopedia classes. Adaptations such as those we witnessed in Toronto by Jane Bancroft and her colleagues at Scarborough College, University of Toronto, showed a wide and diversified range of techniques unattested to in Lozanov's writings. We have tried here to characterize a class as described in the Suggestopedia literature while pointing out where the actual classes we have observed varied considerably from the description.

Bancroft (1972) notes that the four-hour language class has three distinct parts. The first part we might call an oral review section. Previously learned material is used as the basis for discussion by the teacher and twelve students in the class. All participants sit in a circle in their specially designed chairs, and the discussion proceeds like a seminar. This session may involve what are called micro-studies and macro-studies. In micro-studies specific attention is given to grammar, vocabulary, and precise questions and answers. A question from a micro-study might be, "What should one do in a hotel room if the bathroom taps are not working?" In the macro-studies, emphasis is on role playing and wider-ranging, innovative language constructions. "Describe to someone the Boyana church" (one of Bulgaria's most well-known medieval churches) would be an example of a request for information from the macro-studies.

In the second part of the class new material is presented and discussed. This consists of looking over a new dialogue and its native language translation and discussing any issues of grammar, vocabulary, or content that the teacher feels important or that students are curious about. Bancroft notes that this section is typically conducted in the target language, although student questions or comments will be in whatever language the student feels he or she can handle. Students are led to view the experience of dealing with the new material as interesting and undemanding of any special effort or anxiety. The teacher's attitude and authority is considered critical to preparing students for success in the learning to come. The pattern of learning and use is noted (i.e., fixation, reproduction, and new creative production), so that students will know what is expected.

The third part – the seance or concert session – is the one by which Suggestopedia is best known. Since this constitutes the heart of the method, we will quote Lozanov as to how this session proceeds.

At the beginning of the session, all conversation stops for a minute or two, and the teacher listens to the music coming from a tape-recorder. He waits and listens to several passages in order to enter into the mood of the music and then begins to read or recite the new text, his voice modulated in harmony with the musical phrases. The students follow the text in their textbooks where each lesson is translated into the mother tongue. Between the first and second part of the concert, there are several minutes of solemn silence. In some cases, even longer pauses can be given to permit the students to stir a little. Before the beginning of the second part of the concert, there are again several minutes of silence and some phrases of the music are heard again before the teacher begins to read the text. Now the students close their textbooks and listen to the teacher's reading. At the end, the students silently leave the room. They are not told to do any homework on the lesson they have just had except for reading it cursorily once before going to bed and again before getting up in the morning. (Lozanov 1978: 272)

Conclusion

Suggestopedia has probably received both the most enthusiastic and the most critical response of any of the so-called new methods. A rave review appeared in *Parade* magazine of March 12, 1978. Since *Parade* has a weekly circulation of some 30 million Americans, the story on Suggestopedia probably constituted the single largest promotion of foreign language teaching ever. Suggestopedia also received a scathing review in the *TESOL Quarterly*, a journal of somewhat more restricted circulation than *Parade* (Scovel 1979). Having acknowledged that "there are techniques and procedures in Suggestopedy that may prove useful in a foreign language classroom," Scovel notes that Lozanov is unequivocally opposed to any eclectic use of the techniques outside of the full panoply of suggestopedic science. Of suggestopedic science Scovel comments, "If we have learnt anything at all in the seventies, it is that the art of language teaching will benefit very little from the pseudo-science of suggestology" (Scovel 1979: 265).

Scovel takes special issue with Lozanov's use (and misuse) of scholarly citations, terminological jargon, and experimental data and states that "a careful reading of [*Suggestology and Outlines of Suggestopedy*] reveals that there is precious little in suggestology which is scientific" (1979: 257). And yet from Lozanov's point of view, this air of science (rather than its substance) is what gives Suggestopedia its authority in the eyes of students and prepares them to expect success. Lozanov makes no bones about the fact that Suggestopedia is introduced to students in the context of a "suggestive-desuggestive ritual placebo- systems" (Lozanov 1978: 267), and that one of the tasks of the suggestopedic leader is to determine which current ritual placebo system carries most authority with students. The ritual placebo system might be yoga, it might be hypnosis, it might be biofeedback, it might be experimental science. "Ritual placebo systems will change dramatically in accordance with the times. Their desuggestive-suggestive strength weakens with the years. New times create conditions for building up new desuggestive-suggestive ritual 'placebo' systems" (Lozanov 1978: 267). Just as doctors tell patients that the placebo is a pill that will cure them, so teachers tell students that Suggestology is a science that will teach them. And Lozanov maintains that placebos do both cure and teach when the patient or pupil credits them with the power to do so.

Perhaps, then, it is not productive to futher belabor the science/nonscience, data/double-talk issues and instead, as Bancroft and Stevick have done, try to identify and validate those techniques from Suggestopedia that appear effective and that harmonize with other successful techniques in the language teaching inventory.

Bibliography

Bancroft, W. J. 1972. The psychology of suggestopedia or learning without stress. *The Educational Courier* Feb.: 16–19.

Bancroft, W. J. 1978. The Lozanov method and its American adaptions. *Modern Language Journal* 62(4): 167–75.

Blair, R. W. (ed.). 1982 *Innovative Approaches to Language Teaching*. Rowley, Mass.: Newbury House.

Gaston, E. T. (ed.). 1968. *Music in Therapy*. New York: Macmillan.

Hammerly, H. 1982. *Synthesis in Second Language Teaching*. British Columbia: Second Language Publications.

Lozanov, G. 1978. *Suggestology and Outlines of Suggestopedy*. New York: Gordon and Breach.

Ostrander, S., L. Schroeder, and N. Ostrander. 1979. *Superlearning*. New York: Dell.

Scovel, T. 1979. Review of *Suggestology and Outlines of Suggestopedy*. *TESOL Quarterly* 13: 255–66.

Stevick, E. W. 1976. *Memory, Meaning and Method: Some Psychological Perspectives on Language Learning*. Rowley, Mass: Newbury House.

Stevick, E. W. 1980. *Teaching Languages: A Way and Ways*. Rowley, Mass: Newbury House.

11 Comparing and evaluating methods: some suggestions

In the preceding chapters of this book we have examined the fundamental characteristics of eight language teaching proposals in terms of approach, design, and procedure. The use of a common model for the analysis of different teaching philosophies has enabled us to define elements that are common to all approaches and methods and to highlight areas where approaches and methods differ. We have seen that in some cases (e.g., Communicative Language Teaching) teaching proposals have not necessarily led to a specific and well-defined method. In other cases (e.g., Silent Way) there is much less room for interpretation, and explicit specifications may be given for classroom practices.

One level of application of this model is in the comparison of methods. One might wish to know, for instance, if the procedures of two methods are likely to be compatible in the classroom or if two methods share a similar set of underlying theoretical assumptions. As an example, let us use the model to compare Total Physical Response (TPR) and Community Language Learning (CLL).

Comparing methods

Superficially, Total Physical Response and Community Language Learning seem antithetical. Comparing elements at the level of design, we find that TPR typically has a written syllabus with paced introduction of structures and vocabulary. CLL has no syllabus and operates out of what learners feel they need to know. In TPR, the teacher's role is one of drill master, director, and motivator. In CLL, the teacher/knower is counselor, supporter, and facilitator. TPR learners are physically active and mobile. CLL learners are sedentary and in a fixed configuration. TPR assumes no particular relationship among learners and emphasizes the importance of individuals acting alone. CLL is rooted, as its title suggests, in a communal relationship between learners and teachers acting supportively and in concert. At the level of procedure, we find that TPR language practice is largely mechanical, with much emphasis on listening. CLL language practice is innovative, with emphasis on production.

There are elements of commonality, however, which can be easily

154

overlooked. In approach, both TPR and CLL see stress, defensiveness, and embarrassment as the major blocks to successful language learning. They both see the learners' commitment, attention, and group participation as central to overcoming these barriers. They both view the stages of adult language learning as recapitulations of the stages of childhood learning, and both CLL and TPR consider mediation, memory, and recall of linguistic elements to be central issues. TPR holds with CLL that learning is multimodal – that "more involvement must be provided the student than simply sitting in his seat and passively listening. He must be somatically or physiologically, as well as intellectually, engaged" (Curran 1976: 79). At the level of design, neither TPR nor CLL assumes method-specific materials, but both assume that materials can be locally produced as needed.

Other points of comparison between approaches and methods emerge from the use of the present model of analysis. Although we have seen that all approaches and methods imply decisions about both the content of instruction and how content will be taught, methods and approaches differ in the emphasis and priority they give to content versus instructional issues. For example, the Audiolingual Method and some of the versions of Communicative Language Teaching we have considered are all language teaching proposals that see content variables as crucial to successful language teaching. Each makes concrete proposals for a language syllabus, and the syllabus forms the basis for subsequently determined instructional procedures. They differ in what they see as the essential components of a syllabus – since they derive from different views of the nature of language – but each sees a syllabus as a primary component of a language course. On the other hand, such methods as the Silent Way, Counseling-Learning, the Natural Approach, and Total Physical Response start not with language content but rather with a theory of learning. Each is the outcome and application of a particular theory of language learning and an accompanying body of instructional theory. Content considerations are of secondary importance.

But an approach or method is more than simply a set of instructional practices based on a particular view of language and language learning. Implicit in a method are the claims that (a) the method brings about effective second or foreign language learning and (b) it will do so more efficiently than other methods. But in order to assess the value or effectiveness of methods, it is necessary to consider them in relation to a language course or program having specific goals, objectives, and characteristics. In the remainder of this chapter we will outline a basis for evaluating the claims of methods by locating them within the broader context of language curriculum development.

Methods and language curriculum development

From the perspective of language curriculum development, choice of teaching method is but one phase within a system of interrelated curriculum development activities. Choice of teaching approach or method, materials, and learning activities is usually made within the context of language program design and development. When the director of a language school or institution announces to the staff that an incoming client group will consist of forty-five Japanese businessmen requiring a six-week intensive course in spoken English, the teachers will not leap to their feet and exclaim "Let's use Silent Way!" or "Let's use Total Physical Response!" Questions of immediate concern will focus on who the learners are, what their current level of language proficiency is, what sort of communicative needs they have, the circumstances in which they will be using English in the future, and so on. Answers to such questions must be made before program objectives can be established and before choice of syllabus, method, or teaching materials can be made. Such information provides the basis for language curriculum development. Curriculum development requires needs analysis, development of goals and objectives, selection of teaching and learning activities, and evaluation of the outcomes of the language program. Let us consider each of these briefly (for a fuller discussion see Richards 1984).

NEEDS ANALYSIS

Needs analysis is concerned with identifying general and specific language needs that can be addressed in developing goals, objectives, and content in a language program. Needs analysis may focus either on the general parameters of a language program (e.g., by obtaining data on who the learners are, their present level of language proficiency, teacher and learner goals and expectations, the teacher's teaching skills and level of proficiency in the target language, constraints of time and budget, available instructional resources, as well as societal expectations) or on a specific need, such as the kind of listening comprehension training needed for foreign students attending graduate seminars in biology. Needs analysis focuses on what the learner's present level of proficiency is and on what the learner will be required to use the language for on completion of the program. Its aim is to identify the type of language skills and level of language proficiency the program should aim to deliver. Needs analysis acknowledges that the goals of learners vary and must be determined before decisions about content and method can be made. This contrasts with the assumption underlying many methods, namely, that the needs and goals of learners are identical, that what they need is simply "language," and that Method X is the best way to teach it.

FORMULATION OF OBJECTIVES

Information obtained from needs analysis is used in developing, selecting, or revising program objectives. Objectives detail the goals of a language program. They identify the kind and level of language proficiency the learner will attain in the program (if the program is successful). Sometimes program objectives may be stated in terms of a proficiency level in a particular skill area or in the form of behavioral objectives (descriptions of the behaviors or kinds of performance the learners will be able to demonstrate on completion of the program, the conditions under which such performance will be expected to occur, and the criteria used to assess successful performance). The American Council on the Teaching of Foreign Languages has developed provisional proficiency guidelines for use in planning foreign language programs – "a series of descriptions of proficiency levels for speaking, listening, reading, writing, and culture in a foreign language. These guidelines represent a graduated sequence of steps that can be used to structure a foreign-language program" (Liskin-Gasparro 1984: 11).

Decisions about program goals and objectives, whether expressed in terms of behavioral objectives, proficiency levels, or some other form, are essential in language program design. Without clear statements of objectives, questions of content, teaching and learning activities and experiences, materials, and evaluation cannot be systematically addressed. In cases where a specific method is being considered for use in a language program, it is necessary for the program planner to know what the objectives of the method are and the kinds of language proficiencies it seeks to develop. The program planner can then compare the degree of fit between the method and the program goals. However, methods typically fail to describe explicitly the objectives they are designed to attain, leaving teachers and learners to try to infer objectives from the materials and classroom activities themselves.

SELECTION OF TEACHING AND LEARNING ACTIVITIES

Once decisions have been made about the kinds and levels of language proficiency the program is designed to bring about, teaching and learning activities can be chosen. Classroom activities and materials are hence accountable to goals and objectives and are selected according to how well they address the underlying linguistic skills and processes learners will need in order to attain the objectives of the program, that is, to acquire specified skills and behaviors or to attain a particular level of language proficiency. At this phase in language curriculum development, teachers and program developers first select different kinds of tasks, activities, and learning experiences, the effectiveness of which they then test in meeting program goals. This activity is often referred to as the domain of methodology in language teaching. It involves experimentation, informed by the current state of the art in second language learning theory, and research into the teaching and learning of reading, writing, listening, speaking. Curriculum developers typically proceed with caution, since there is a great deal that is unknown about second language acquisition and little justification for uncritical adoption of rigid proposals.

At this phase in curriculum development, choice of a particular method can be justified only when it is clear that there is a close degree of fit between the program goals and objectives and the objectives of the method. Information concerning the kinds of gains in language proficiency that the method has been shown to bring about in similar circumstances would also be needed here, if available. When a close degree of fit between method and program objectives is lacking, a choice can be made through "informed eclecticism." By this we mean that various design features and procedures are selected, perhaps drawn from different methods, that can be shown to relate explicitly to program objectives. Most language teaching programs operate from a basis of informed eclecticism rather than by attempting to rigidly implement a specific method. A policy of uninformed eclecticism (which is how the term *eclectic* or *eclectic method* is often used), on the other hand, would be where techniques, activities, and features from different methods are selected without explicit reference to program objectives.

EVALUATION

Evaluation refers to procedures for gathering data on the dynamics, effectiveness, acceptability, and efficiency of a language program for the purposes of decision making. Basically, evaluation addresses whether the goals and objectives of a language program are being attained, that is, whether the program is effective (in absolute terms). In cases where a choice must be made between two possible program options geared to the same objectives, a secondary focus may be on the relative effectiveness of the program. In addition, evaluation may be concerned with how teachers, learners, and materials interact in classrooms, and how teachers and learners perceive the program's goals, materials, and learning experiences. The relatively short life span of most language teaching methods and the absence of a systematic approach to language program development in many language teaching institutions is largely attributable to inadequate allowance for program evaluation in the planning process. In the absence of a substantial database informing decisions

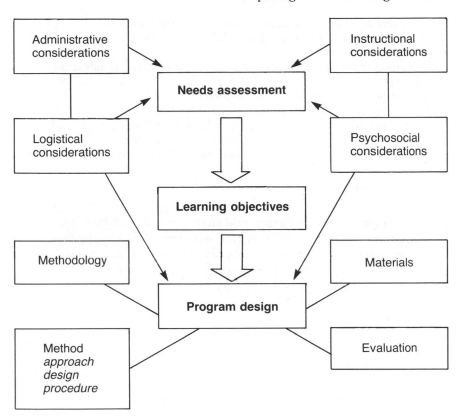

Figure 11.1 Language curriculum development processes

about how effective a language program is or how its results are achieved, chance and fashion alone often determine program adoption and adaptation. Consequently much has been written about the design of language teaching courses, methods, syllabuses, and materials, but little has been published about the impact on learners of programs, approaches, methods, instructional strategies, and materials. The relationship of the different components of language curriculum development are summarized in Figure 11.1. In order to illustrate relevant issues in the evaluation of methods, we will outline the different dimensions of evaluation that could be applied to the approaches and methods we have discussed in this book.

Evaluating methods

If adequate evaluation data were available about the methods we have analyzed, we could expect to find answers to such general questions as

What aspects of language proficiency does the method address?
With what kinds of learners (children, adults, etc.) is the method most
  effective?
Is the method most effective with elementary, intermediate, or advanced
  learners?
What kind of training is required of teachers?
Under what circumstances does the method work best? (E.g., has it been
  found to be effective with learners from different cultural backgrounds?)
How have teachers and students responded to the method?
How does the method compare with other methods (e.g., when used to attain
  a specified type of competency)?
Do teachers using the method use it in a uniform manner?

Answers to questions like these would enable decisions to be made about
the relevance of specific methods to particular kinds of language programs. In order to answer these kinds of questions we look to four kinds
of data: descriptive data, observational data, effectiveness data, and
comparative data. Let us consider each of these in turn.

Descriptive data

Descriptive data are objective (as far as possible) descriptions and accounts, usually by teachers, of specific procedures used in teaching according to a particular method. They may take the form of amplified
records of lesson plans, with detailed comments on the exact steps followed. Evaluation specialists sometimes refer to these as "thick descriptions," by which is meant "literal description of the activity being
evaluated, the circumstances under which it is used, the characteristics
of the people involved in it, the nature of the community in which it is
located, and the like" (Guba and Lincoln 1981: 119). David Cohen
refers to the use of such descriptions in foreign language teaching as

detailed first person description... that fixes vivid perceptions in time and
prevents their deterioration into TEFL folklore and even myth. Such a history
of a teaching year is of applied value both pedagogically in the language
classroom and in terms of an ordered system of guided curriculum development. It provides a reliable "organizational memory" and, over time, becomes the framework for an integrative longitudinal analysis of student
cohorts as they move from level to level within the ability streams of an on-
going English language program. (Cohen 1984: 30)

Sylvia Ashton-Warner's book *Teacher* exemplifies many of the characteristics of "thick description." Here is part of her commentary on the
use of key vocabulary in teaching reading.

The words, which I write on large tough cards and give to the children to
read, prove to be one-look words if they are accurately enough chosen. And

they are plain enough in conversation. It's the conversation that has to be got. However, if it can't be, I find that whatever a child chooses to make in the creative period may quite likely be such a word. But if the vocabulary of a child is still inaccessible, one can always begin him on the general Key Vocabulary, common to any child in any race, a set of words bound up with security that experiments, and later on their creative writing, show to be organically associated with the inner world: "Mommy," "Daddy," "kiss," "frightened," "ghost."

"Mohi," I ask a new five, an undisciplined Maori, "what word do you want?"

"Jet!"

I smile and write it on a strong little card and give it to him. "What is it again?"

"Jet!"

"You can bring it back in the morning. What do you want, Gay?"

Gay is the classic overdisciplined bullied victim of the respectable mother.

"House," she whispers. So I write that, too, and give it into her eager hand.

"What do you want, Seven?" Seven is a violent Maori.

"Bomb! Bomb! I want bomb!"

So Seven gets his word "bomb" and challenges anyone to take it from him.

And so on through the rest of them. They ask for a new word each morning and never have I to repeat to them what it is. And if you saw the condition of these tough little cards the next morning you'd know why they need to be of tough cardboard or heavy drawing paper rather than thin paper.

(Ashton-Warner 1965: 32–3)

We have found that for most of the approaches and methods we have reviewed, there is a lack of detailed description. Most methods exist primarily as proposals, and we have no way of knowing how they are typically implemented by teachers. The protocols in the procedure section of each chapter represent an attempt to provide at least partial descriptions of how methods are used in the classroom.

Observational data

Observational data refer to recorded observations of methods as they are being taught. Such data can be used to evaluate whether the method as it is implemented actually conforms to its underlying philosophy or approach. The observer is typically not the teacher, but a trained observer with a note pad, tape recorder, video equipment, or some other means of capturing the moment-to-moment behaviors of teachers and learners in the classroom. Gathering observational data is much more problematical than obtaining descriptive data, but ultimately more essential, since it provides a more accurate record of what actually occurred, relying as it does on an outsider's observations rather than on what the teacher thought occurred or should occur. Classroom observation studies are a well-established and reasonably noncontroversial part of educational reporting in other fields, and we should expect reports in language teaching to be equivalent in quality to those in general education. Studies carried out in L2 classrooms in recent years have highlighted the potential contribution of observational studies to method evaluation.

Long and Sato (1984), for example, looked at language use in classes taught by teachers trained in "communicative" methodology and compared it with the language of real communication outside of classrooms (native speakers addressing nonnatives of the same level of proficiency as the classroom learners). They found the type of language used by the "communicative" teachers to be very different from the language of natural communication outside the classroom. The teachers' language shared many of the features of the mechanical question-and-answer drills characteristic of audiolingual classrooms. Such studies emphasize the need for empirical study of the classroom processes (i.e., the types of interactions between learners and learners, learners and teachers, learners and materials) as well as the classroom discourse (i.e., the types of utterances, question-and-answer exchanges, turn taking, feedback, and so on) that characterize methods as they are actually used in the classroom, as opposed to how they are described by writers on methods. Observed differences between methods at the level of classroom processes and classroom discourse may be less marked than differences at the descriptive or theoretical level.

Swaffar, Arens, and Morgan (1982), for example, conducted a study of differences between what they termed rationalist and empiricist approaches to foreign language instruction. By a rationalist approach they refer to process-oriented approaches in which language learning is seen as an interrelated whole, where language learning is a function of comprehension preceding production, and where it involves critical thinking and the desire to communicate. Empiricist approaches focus on the four discrete language skills. Would such differences be reflected in differences in classroom practices?

One consistent problem is whether or not teachers involved in presenting materials created for a particular method are actually reflecting the underlying philosophies of these methods in their classroom practices. (Swaffar et al. 1982: 25)

Swaffar et al. found that many of the distinctions used to contrast methods, particularly those based on classroom activities, did not exist in actual practice.

Methodological labels assigned to teaching activities are, in themselves, not informative, because they refer to a pool of classroom practices which are used uniformly. The differences among major methodologies are to be found in the ordered hierarchy, the priorities assigned to tasks. (1982: 31)

The implications of these findings for the study of methods are profound. They suggest that differences among methods of the kind highlighted in the present analysis need to be complemented by observational studies of methods as they are implemented in classrooms. For example, what kinds of techniques and strategies do teachers operating with different methods use for such tasks as clarifying meanings of words, eliciting repetition, giving feedback, correcting errors, giving directions, and controlling learner behavior? What patterns of turn taking are observed? What is the nature of teacher and learner discourse, both quantitatively and qualitatively, and how do these, as well as the other features noted here, vary according to level? We know a great deal about methods and approaches at the level of philosophy and belief, that is, in terms of how the advocates of a particular method believe a method or technique should be used; but few data are available on what actually happens to methods when teachers use them in the classroom. It is no exaggeration to say that in reality, there is virtually no literature on the Natural Approach, Communicative Language Teaching, the Silent Way, and so on; what we have is a number of books and articles on the theory of these methods and approaches, but almost nothing on how such theory is reflected in actual classroom practices and processes. Hence the crucial question is, Do methods really exist in terms of classroom practices, or do teachers, when using methods, in fact transform them into more complex but less distinctive patterns of classroom processes?

Effectiveness data

The third kind of information needed is data on the extent to which particular methods have been found to be effective. What is needed minimally for specific methods is (1) documented studies of instances where a method has been used with reference to a specific set of objectives and (2) reliable and valid measures of gains in proficiency made by learners relative to the objectives. Our profession will indicate its maturity by means of the candor with which we are able to design, carry out, and report measures of effectiveness in something like normal teaching circumstances. The need to provide such data is considered normal in most other areas of educational planning, but data of this kind are virtually nonexistant in the literature on language teaching methods. It is surely not too much to demand of method promoters documentation of instances where students have made gains in proficiency from being taught according to a particular approach or method. To demonstrate this, it is necessary not only to compare pretest and posttest results (and state clearly *what* is being tested) but to show that the results were achieved as a result of method rather than despite it.

The St. Lambert French immersion program in Canada offers perhaps the closest one can come to a model evaluation study of this kind. In that project, a reasonably large number of students have been followed longitudinally over a six-year period, and their language progress and language attitudes have been measured against the standard of cohort groups of monolingual French and monolingual English students. An outline of the domains of the evaluation and summary statements of results in four of the domains will suffice to suggest the findings:

The evaluation covered seven separate domains:

1. English language arts.
2. French language arts.
3. French-and-English-speaking skills.
4. French phonology.
5. Achievement in content subjects.
6. Intelligence.
7. Attitudes toward French Canadians, English Canadians, European French, and self.

In the area of English Language Arts (as measured by the Metropolitan Achievement Tests and the Peabody Vocabulary Test), the students in the experimental class performed as well as their English peers who had been educated in their native language.

In the area of French Language Arts, the bilingual students when compared with native French-speaking students are somewhat behind in vocabulary knowledge; write compositions in French which, although they contain no more grammatical errors, are less rich in content; and score at approximately the 60th percentile on a test of French achievement.

When asked to tell in English about a film they had been shown, the bilingual students performed similarly to their English instructed counterparts on all measures taken which included the number of episodes, details, and inferences recounted, as well as the number of false starts, grammatical self-corrections, and content self-corrections made. When asked to tell in French about the film, the bilingual students made more grammatical and content self-corrections than native French students but otherwise performed similarly to them.

A number of phonological traits not characteristic of French native speakers were noted in the speech of many of the bilingual children. They included the diphthongization of the mid-vowels, the aspiration of voiceless stops, and inappropriate placing of stress on the first syllable. (Swain and Barik 1978: 33)

Comparative data

The most difficult kind of data to provide is that which offers evidence that one method is more effective than another in attaining program objectives. St. Pierre (1979) describes the conventional method for such evaluations:

Both experimental and quasi-experimental evaluations exhibit many of the same ideal characteristics. Program goals subject to evaluation are selected, success criteria are stated, measures are selected/constructed, an evaluation design is developed, treatment and comparison groups are formed, data are collected and analyzed, conclusions about the effectiveness of the program are drawn, and a report is written. (St. Pierre 1979: 29)

However, the history of attempts at method comparisons should be kept in mind. Since the 1950s a number of ambitious attempts have been made at testing the comparative effectiveness of methods. Most often, researchers have been unable to demonstrate the effectiveness of specific methods. For example, a major large-scale investigation of the Audiolingual Method (Smith 1970), like other methods studies before it, failed to demonstrate that the Audiolingual Method had any significant impact on improvement of language learning. As Kennedy observes,

The repeatedly ambiguous results of these and other attempts to demonstrate experimentally the superiority of one or another foreign language teaching method suggest, it would seem, not only that it is extremely difficult to compare methods experimentally, but, more important, that methodology may not be the critical variable in successful foreign language teaching. (Kennedy 1973: 68)

Critics of the conventional model have noted that "not all sciences are experimental; not all aspire to be. An approach to evaluation that stresses the experimental test of causes is not ipso facto a more scientific approach" (Glass and Ellett 1980: 223).

One way to minimize the difficulties of large-scale comparative method evaluations is through studies that are much more restricted in scope. An example of an evaluation of this kind is a study by Wagner and Tilwey (1983). The method they examined was derived from Suggestopedia (Lozanov 1978) and Superlearning (Ostrander, Schroeder, and Ostrander 1979). Advocates of Superlearning claim that learners can learn 2,000 lexical items in twenty-three hours by studying just three hours a day. Wagner and Tilney designed a study to evaluate these claims. In their study, twenty-one subjects were randomly assigned to one of three experimental treatments or modes of vocabulary presentation. The experimental group received German language training with Superlearning methodology. A second group received the same Superlearning methodology but without the use of Baroque music – the use of which is a key feature of Lozanov's method. A third group received language training in the classroom and served as a no-contact control group. Levels of vocabulary learning in each group were compared. The results revealed no significant improvement across the five-week experimental period. When modes of presentation were compared, those subjects taught by a traditional classroom method learned significantly more vocabulary than those taught according to Superlearning principles. Although this study contained a very limited number of subjects, it suggests how specific claims of a method can be tested before a commitment is made to implementation on a wider scale.

None of the four levels of evaluation we have described here can be considered sufficient in itself. Descriptive data often lack reliability; they record impressions and recollections rather than facts. Observational data record processes and interactions but do not enable us to determine how these affect learning outcomes. Effectiveness data record results, but do not always tell us how or why these results were brought about. Comparative data likewise compare outcomes, but fail to take account of processes and actual classroom behaviors. The need for an integrated approach to evaluation is consequently stressed:

1. Evaluation...can be seen as a continuing part of management rather than as a short-term consulting contract. 2. The evaluator, instead of running alongside the train making notes through the windows, can board the train and influence the engineer, the conductor and the passengers. 3. The evaluator need not limit his concerns to objectives stated in advance; instead he can also function as a naturalistic observer whose enquiries grow out of his observations. 4. The evaluator should not concentrate on outcomes; ultimately it may prove more profitable to study just what was delivered and how people interacted during the treatment process. 5. The evaluator should recognize (and act upon the recognition) that systems are rarely influenced by reports in the mail. (Ross and Cronbach 1976: 18)

Unfortunately, evaluation data of any kind are all too rare in the vast promotional literature on methods. Too often, techniques and instructional philosophies are advocated from a philosophical or theoretical stance rather than on the basis of any form of evidence. Hence, despite the amount that has been written about methods and teaching techniques, serious study of methods, either in terms of curriculum development practice or as classroom processes, has hardly begun. Few method writers locate methods within curriculum development, that is, within an integrated set of processes that involve systematic data gathering, planning, experimentation, and evaluation. A method proposal is typically a rationale for techniques of presentation and practice of language items. Seldom is it accompanied by an examination of outcomes or classroom processes. Language teaching has evolved a considerable body of educational techniques, and the quest for the ideal method is part of this tradition. The adoption of an integrated and systematic approach to language curriculum processes underscores the limitations of such a quest and emphasizes the need to develop a more rigorous basis for our educational practice.

Bibliography

Ashton-Warner, S. 1965. *Teacher*. New York: Bantam.

Cohen, D. N. 1984. Historical TEFL: a case study. *RELC Journal* 51(1): 30–50.

Curran, C. 1976. *Counseling-Learning in Second Languages*. Apple River, Ill.: Apple River Press.

Glass, G. V., and F. S. Ellett. 1980. Evaluation research. *Annual Review of Psychology* 31: 211–28.

Guba, E. G., and Y. S. Lincoln. 1981. *Effective Evaluation: Improving the Usefulness of Evaluation Results Through Responsive and Naturalistic Approaches*. San Francisco: Jossey-Bass.

Kennedy, G. 1973. Conditions for language learning. In J. W. Oller and J. C. Richards (eds.), *Focus on the Learner*, pp. 66–80. Rowley, Mass.: Newbury House.

Liskin-Gasparro, J. 1984. The ACTFL proficiency guidelines: an historical perspective. In T. Higgs (ed.), *Teaching for Proficiency*, pp. 11–42. Lincolnwood, Ill.: National Textbook Co.

Long, M. H. 1984. Process and product in ESL program evaluation. *TESOL Quarterly* 18(3): 409–25.

Long, M. H., and C. Sato. 1983. Classroom foreigner talk discourse; forms and functions of teacher's questions. In H. Seliger and M. Long (eds.), *Classroom Oriented Research in Second Language Acquisition*, pp. 268–86. Rowley, Mass.: Newbury House.

Lozanov, G. 1978. *Suggestology and Outlines of Suggestopedy*. New York: Gordon and Breach.

Ostrander, S., L. Schroeder, and N. Ostrander. 1979. *Superlearning*. New York: Dell.

Richards, J. C. 1984. Language curriculum development. *RELC Journal* 15(1): 1–29.

Ross, L., and L. J. Cronbach. 1976. Review of the *Handbook of Evaluation Research*. *Educational Researcher* 5(9): 9–19.

Smith, P. D. Jr. 1970. *A Comparison of the Cognitive and Audiolingual Approaches to Foreign Language Instruction*. Philadelphia: Center for Curriculum Development.

Swaffar, J. K., K. Arens, and M. Morgan. 1982. Teacher classroom practices: redefining method as task hierarchy. *The Modern Language Journal* 66(1): 24–33.

St. Pierre, R. G. 1979. The role of multiple analyses in quasi-experimental evaluations. *Educational Evaluation and Policy Analysis* 1(6): 5–10.

Swain, M., and H. Barik. 1978. Bilingual education in Canada: French and English. In B. Spolsky and R. Cooper (eds.), *Case Studies in Bilingual Education*, pp. 22–71. Rowley, Mass.: Newbury House.

Wagner, M. J., and G. Tilney. 1983. The effect of "superlearning techniques" on the vocabulary acquisition and alpha brainwave production of language learners. *TESOL Quarterly* 17(1): 5–19.

Index

169

Index

170